From Cost Center to Value Center

From Cost Center to Value Center

Making the Move to Utility Computing

by

Dr. Guy Bunker
Tim Coulter
Charles Hart
Evan Marcus
Mark Seager
Dr. Barry Steer
Edited by Evan Marcus and Paul Massiglia
Glossary by Paula Skoe
With artwork by Charlie Van Meter and Bob Santiago
Project managed by Ramesh Kumar and Paula Skoe

VERITAS Software Corporation

Project Managers: Ramesh Kumar and Paula Skoe
Editors: Evan Marcus and Paul Massiglia
Glossary: Paula Skoe
Artwork: Charlie Van Meter and Bob Santiago

Library of Congress Control Number: 2003113822

Printed in the United States of America.

VERITAS Software Corporation
350 Ellis Street
Mountain View, CA 94043

ISBN: 0-974-4578-1-7
1 2 3 4 5 6 7 8 9 10—CDS—07 06 05 04 03 02 01
www.VERITAS.com

u·til·i·ty ***(y›-t¹l“¹-t¶)*** ***n., pl.*** ***u·til·i·ties.*** ***1. The quality or condition of being useful; usefulness: “I have always doubted the utility of these conferences on disarmament” (Winston S. Churchill).*** **2.** ***A useful article or device.*** **3.** ***Abbr.*** **util.** **a.** ***A public utility.*** **b.** ***A commodity or service, such as electricity, water, or public transportation, that is provided by a public utility.***

— The American Heritage Dictionary

About the Authors

Dr. Guy Bunker is Director of Strategic Engineering at VERITAS Software Corporation. Guy has been a member of a number of industry bodies and is currently a member of the Global Grid Forum's Grid Market Awareness Council. Dr. Bunker holds a Ph.D. in Artificial Neural Networks from King's College London.

Tim Coulter is the Technical Product Manager for UNIX Replication at VERITAS. He has implemented many of the technologies discussed in this book for companies around the world. Mr. Coulter has pursued knowledge in many institutes of higher education, including but not limited to Grossmont City College, De Anza City College, San Jose State University, and the University of California San Diego, and he has completed additional coursework in a number of technical schools.

Charles Hart is a 20-year veteran of large-scale IT shops where he has worked to create services and the tools to administer them. In his IT career he has held a wide variety of positions, including advanced technology specialist, consultant, analyst, programmer, designer, database administrator, system administrator, network manager, and operations manager. In his latest role as Senior Director of Management Products at VERITAS, he helps deliver innovative storage and service management products for enterprise data centers. Mr. Hart holds a B.A. in English from Boston College.

Evan Marcus is a principal engineer at VERITAS. An expert on data availability, he is coauthor of *Blueprints for High Availability* (2nd Edition, September 2003); he also frequently writes and lectures on the design of high availability systems. Mr. Marcus has a B.S. in Computer Science from Lehigh University and an M.B.A. from Rutgers University.

Mark Seager is the Senior Director of Technology across EMEA for VERITAS. With nearly 20 years IT experience, Mark has worked for GEC Avionics where he designed real-time, fault-tolerant flight control systems for both military and commercial customers. He has also worked as Kernel Developer for leading RDBMS developer Cincom Systems. Prior to joining VERITAS, he ran the London-based Open Systems division for Nikko Europe. Mr. Seager has a degree in Computer Science, which was sponsored by GEC Avionics.

Dr. Barry Steer is Principal Applications and Technology Architect within Information Systems and Technology at VERITAS. He is an architecture expert who has consulted and held architecture and software engineering positions at Visa International, Hewlett-Packard, Raytheon, and Scientific Atlanta. He also served a four-year engineering apprenticeship with ITT and has spoken at the National Academy of Sciences in Washington, D.C. Dr. Steer holds a Ph.D. in Computer Science and carried out postdoctoral research work at Oxford University.

The Editors

This book was edited by Evan Marcus and Paul Massiglia. Biographical information for Evan Marcus can be found under "About the Authors."

Paul Massiglia is a Technical Director of Engineering at VERITAS. He has written and edited numerous volumes on storage technologies and disaster recovery, including *Virtual Storage Redefined: Technologies and Applications for Storage Virtualization*. Mr. Massiglia holds a B.S.C.S., summa cum laude, from Colorado Technical University.

Contents

Figures

Tables

Foreword

Today, chief information officers face a dilemma. As corporate executives, they must contribute to the bottom line by keeping the cost of IT services low. But as heads of service organizations, they face increasing demands for more and better service from business lines and operating departments within the enterprise. In essence, CIOs are being asked to do more with less.

VERITAS and other companies in the industry are proposing solutions to this dilemma that we call *utility computing* — adapting techniques employed by utility companies to deliver essential services like electricity, water, and communications to the delivery of information services within a company.

On the surface, utility computing is attractive. By streamlining IT service offerings, enterprises can reduce cost and improve quality of service at the same time. Using a shared delivery infrastructure, they improve utilization and also become more flexible and better able to respond to changing business conditions. By accounting for IT service usage, they better align IT with business objectives.

It's a compelling image, but how do we make it a reality? Many IT companies are articulating utility computing visions, but few are explaining the critical building blocks necessary to implement a utility model for IT, and even fewer are telling their customers how to implement the concept. For this reason, I commissioned a team of our top engineers, product managers, consultants, and representatives of our own IT department to write this book.

I asked our people to describe in detail what we as a company mean by utility computing. I asked them to articulate the benefits of adopting the IT utility model, and most important, I asked them to present a blueprint for implementation — to explain how an IT organization can transform itself from conventional data processing into an IT utility that delivers improved service levels at lower cost through automation of a shared infrastructure.

This book begins by enumerating the essential characteristics of a utility and focuses on those that are relevant to information technology. It describes how an ideal IT utility would operate and goes on to suggest how an enterprise can consider the benefits of utility computing, how to make the transition, and what outcomes can be expected.

This book should interest anyone involved in delivering or using information technology services, but its particular target is IT management, from the system administrator to the CIO. We hope you find it to be informative and a useful tool for guiding your own enterprise along the path to utility computing.

Sincerely,

Gary Bloom
Chairman, President, & CEO,
VERITAS Software Corporation

Acknowledgments

This book could not have come together without the wholehearted support of many committed individuals throughout VERITAS. The authors wish to particularly acknowledge the contributions of Martin Ward for the initial idea and for funding production, and Ramesh Kumar for managing the development. Vitaly Gudanets, Mark Johnson, Hal Uygur, Nick Mehta, Peter Grimmond, Darren Thomson, and David Rogers all made significant contributions and spent what must have seemed like thankless hours in reviewing the manuscript. Karen Ancell managed to capture co-author Mark Seager's wonderfully clear and concise expression of the VERITAS utility computing strategy for posterity. Frank Bunn painstakingly reviewed the manuscript for understandability by non-native English speakers. Jeff Rennacker and Nelson Carnicelli turned a few sound bites into a cover that reflects the spirit of the message, and Leslie Howard capably managed production of the final book.

The VERITAS Publishing model relies on authors who take on writing responsibilities over and above the scope of their day jobs. This model wouldn't work without the enthusiastic support of executive management. We thank Fred van den Bosch, Greg Valdez, Mark Bregman, Mike Tardif, Rick Huebsch, and John Freeman for their support.

Finally, the entire team and VERITAS as a whole owe a debt of gratitude to the vision and foresight of Richard Barker, who in addition to turning an idea into this finished product, oversaw the founding of VERITAS Publishing, so that when the time came to create this book, the machinery was in place to make it happen.

We thank you all.

Guy Bunker
Tim Coulter
Charles Hart
Evan Marcus
Paul Massiglia
Mark Seager
Paula Skoe
Barry Steer
October 15, 2003

Who Should Read This Book and Why

This book is for information technology (IT) managers, general business managers, and other IT professionals interested in increasing the value of IT in their organizations. Its premise is that the most effective way to deliver IT value is to treat its resources and services as commodities delivered on demand, in much the same way that consumer commodities are delivered by utility companies.

It begins by describing the essential characteristics of the utility model for product and service delivery and then examines why some things are delivered by utilities and others are not. Next, it argues that information is best delivered to its users (departments and business units) using techniques similar to those used by the companies that deliver electricity, gas, water, and so forth. Utility-style delivery of information services is more cost effective and generally delivers higher quality of service than conventional delivery models.

With the concept established that information services can be delivered cost effectively by a utility, the book examines the nature of the information service utility — the components that comprise it, the mechanisms for assembling them into a delivery pipeline, and the central issue of managing the pipeline in the context of a complex and rapidly changing business environment.

The book concludes with a discussion of how to get there from here and explains how an enterprise turns a conventional data center that "costs what it costs and does what it does when it does it" into a flexible, reliable, and adaptable value center that is accountable to the users that pay for it.

Anyone who uses information technology to achieve business success should be interested in this book's message. Simply stated, that message is, "Delivery of information services by a utility will result in both cost savings and higher-quality information than delivery by conventional methods."

Introduction

"High availability is just like ordinary availability, only higher."

— Evan Marcus, VERITAS Data Availability Maven

In just a half century, electronic information technology has changed more radically than any other technology in human history. From huge, inflexible machines in "glass houses" accessible only to the largest enterprises, the machines that store and process information have evolved into tens of millions of desktop, notebook, and handheld devices used extensively by average people in their everyday lives. A growing variety of communication technologies connects the visible computers to millions of invisible servers that fulfill requests for the information that has become indispensable to modern life.

Implementing Information Services

Computers and computer networks are probably the most complex and bewildering devices that most people will ever use. Even accomplished computer engineers often find themselves baffled by the behavior of their creations. For tens of millions of lay users, there is no hope of understanding even the most basic workings of the computers and networks that increasingly dominate their lives.

Fortunately, users have no more need to understand the workings of computers to use them than they have to understand how an automatic transmission works in order to drive a car. Information technology (IT) has developed a priesthood of specialists that caters to the needs of the information laity by creating more comprehensive systems, as well as hotlines and help desks that solve the little information problems of daily life.

This priesthood of IT professionals has developed an extensive body of collective knowledge, which has grown into entire university computer science programs, many specializing in information systems. Experienced developers have spent hundreds and thousands of person-years implementing information systems. Major consulting firms collect large fees for applying carefully honed methodologies to solve complex information technology problems.

One would think that an industry so rich in expertise would have developed a clear-cut methodology for building and operating information services, a methodology in which standard solutions to difficult problems are documented, much as they are in home construction or plumbing. Such a methodology would explain which components to install, how to interconnect them, and how to manage them in order to achieve the business goals of the service. With all the accumulated expertise in the field, surely the definitive guide to developing information technology services has been written.

Alas, it has not. Today, the culture of information technology treats each new information system as a journey into the unknown that demands its own requirements gathering, component selection, detailed planning, installation, operational practices, and quality assurance. Two attitudes pervade information system development:

- Every information system has unique requirements.
- Every new information system must be custom-developed by specialists.

While these attitudes may have been valid in the early days of information technology, they are highly questionable today. Consider that:

- With literally millions of information systems in operation around the world, there are, in fact, common principles of operations, security, and data protection that are applied over and over again. Re-creating principles and practices for every new system is wasteful in the extreme.
- As dominant suppliers of common business applications emerge (Oracle for databases, Siebel for customer relationship management, PeopleSoft for human resources, SAP for financials, and so forth), fewer new information systems actually involve application development. Implementation is more likely to consist of customization and deployment of purchased applications. Today, the problems in information service implementation are predictable performance, guaranteed availability, and data protection — quality of service rather than uniqueness of function.
- Individual planning and custom design of information systems flies in the face of today's most compelling business reality — rapid pace of change. The more carefully laid out an information system is, the

less likely it is to be adaptable to changes in requirements, such as a doubling of capacity. A superior approach is to construct services from standard modular building blocks that can be replicated easily as requirements change.

Given these realities of modern information service deployment, one must question whether the old model of custom services implemented by a priesthood using an arcane body of knowledge is still the best one. Could there be a better way?

Introducing Utility Computing

There is, in fact, a better way to develop, deploy, and operate information services — a standardized methodology called *utility computing*. The name utility computing suggests an analogy with other common services such as electricity and water that are delivered as utilities. The analogy is appealing to consumers and producers of information services and the executives who run the organizations that consume the information that the services provide.

- ***To consumers***, it suggests that computing has something in common with things they take for granted as amenities of modern life. Flip the switch, and lights go on. Twist the tap, and water comes out. In computing, click the mouse, and bills are paid, reservations are made, employees are promoted, customers are served — all without thinking about the "wiring and plumbing" that allows it to happen.
- ***To producers***, it suggests that computer-based information services can be deployed, used, managed, and adapted using well-understood techniques similar to those that have evolved for telephone, water, electricity, and similar services. Compared to today's hand-crafted "work of art" information services, the utility model is a manager's dream that will reduce delivery time and manpower requirements and improve the quality of the services delivered.
- ***To executives*** charged with balancing the competitive need for more and better information services against the reality of controlling operating expenses, utility computing offers a ray of hope — information services that *scale*, or grow, to meet growing demand at measurable and understandable cost.

If information services really can be delivered using utility techniques, the implications are significant. From a unique solution to every problem, implemented and maintained by a priesthood of specialists, information technology would become "plumbing" that is just there. Freed from implementing and managing different-every-time services, IT organizations could devote their energies to delivering more services faster using automated infrastructures of standard components. With component and delivery standardization comes measurability and ultimately complete business accountability for IT use.

Can information services be delivered by a utility? Every major information technology supplier today would have users believe so. But beneath the surface, most so-called utility computing architectures are nothing more than computer system architectures. Computer systems are necessary, but without the right techniques for deployment, operation, and accountability, they do not make a utility.

Looking further beneath the surface reveals that systems have been augmented by provisioning, performance monitoring, and resource accounting tools. Management tools are necessary in a utility but do not by themselves achieve the quality, cost, timeliness, and accountability goals of a utility.

The chapters of Part 1 describe a universal model for utility computing that adapts techniques used by companies that deliver common commodities like electricity, gas, and water. They demonstrate that the principles that allow these utility companies to deliver services cost effectively and profitably can be adapted to information service delivery. The methods described are largely independent of specific technology; many different tools can be combined to meet utility computing requirements.

Part 2 enumerates some key areas in which benefits can be realized quickly and suggests a stepwise roadmap for complete conversion to the utility model.

The goal is simple: to persuade the reader that utility computing is a useful paradigm for information service delivery that bears close examination and, for almost all enterprises, adoption.

PART 1

Utilities and Information Technology

The premise of this book is that enterprise information services can be delivered most effectively using delivery techniques similar to those used by electric, gas, telephone, and water utility companies to deliver their products. In this part, we examine what it is that makes a utility a utility and how the concepts used by utility companies to deliver their products and services can be applied to information technology.

CHAPTER 1

The Utility Model

"Men first feel necessity, then look for utility."

— Giambattista Vico

In this chapter...

- Essentials of the utility model
- Benefits and drawbacks of the utility model
- Key properties of a utility

A good starting point for appreciating what an information technology utility does is an understanding of what makes any company a utility.

What Utilities Are

A utility is defined as a business that performs essential public services[1] subject to government regulation.[2] While the utilities' business model, rather than their relationship to governments, is of interest in this book, this definition has four key implications that are relevant when applying the utility model to enterprise computing:

- A utility provides essential services
- A utility provides a small set of services to a large user community
- A utility is reliable
- A utility is a business

1. The business of supplying an essential commodity, such as water or electricity, or a service, such as communications or transportation, to the public. —www.dictionary.com (WordNet® 1.6, © 1997 Princeton University), definition #3.

2. Different countries regulate their utilities differently, even oscillating between public and private corporations at different times. It is generally true, however, that the commodities provided by utilities are regarded as sufficiently vital to be regulated as to price and quality of service.

The sections that follow discuss these four key points.

Essential Services

As society increasingly exploits technology, more and more services join the list of essentials. A century ago, water was an essential service in cities, but electricity and telephone service were luxuries. Fifty years ago, electricity had become essential, and telephone service nearly so. As recently as 20 years ago, broadcast media delivered on cable or by satellite were relative rarities; today, they are well on their way to universal deployment.

Today, computing has become essential to the conduct of business. Without reliable networks, application deployment, data protection, and maintenance, much of business would be impossible to conduct. It is time to consider whether computing should be delivered in the same manner as other essential business services.

A Small Set of Services Supplied to a Large User Community

Utility companies provide relatively simple products or services to large communities of users. A water department provides water. A user's access portal to water may be small (for a home or small business) or large (for an office tower), but the product is the same. Similarly, electric utilities deliver power. Voltage and maximum load may vary, but the service is basically the same for all users. Some utilities deliver commodities that are consumed in quantity, like water, electricity, or gas. Users pay for these in proportion to the amounts consumed. Other utilities, such as cable or satellite broadcast companies, deliver services. The value to the consumer is in having access to the service. With a few notable exceptions (pay-per-view, for example), the amount consumed is irrelevant.

Computing has aspects of both a product and a service. The value of storage capacity and processing is proportional to the quantity of either that is consumed. Other services, like corporate Web access, provide value by being available, no matter how much or how little they are used.

The small set of products offered by a utility and the large size of its user base are important to the model because economy of scale makes it possible to deliver commodities cheaply and reliably. Every house could draw its water from a well and generate its own electricity, but it is impractical to do so. Water can be stored, purified, and piped far more cheaply from a citywide plant, and electricity is more efficiently generated in city-sized quantities.

Similar rules of scale hold for enterprise computing. At first glance, it might appear that many small independent servers can deliver computing capability less expensively than enterprise-class servers. But the capital expense of servers is only the tip of the cost iceberg. Total cost of ownership also includes a proper data center environment, data protection, and professional management. Enterprise computing, like other commodity products and services, is most effectively delivered to large numbers of consumers by a central utility.

Reliable Services

As a service becomes essential, so does the expectation that it will be reliably available. Consider what happens during a power outage. While just about everyone has experienced a power outage, the fact that they are so memorable attests to their rarity. In New York, for example, long-time residents still recall the blackout of 1965. It is likely that the 2003 blackout will be similarly remembered. But while a blackout is in progress, it is a major annoyance.

Society routinely depends on electric power for cooking, cleaning, and entertainment and to run the machines that make it possible to produce, buy, and sell goods and services. Interruption of utility service disrupts that routine; it cannot be tolerated. So governments regulate utilities, and utility companies attach significant urgency to fixing outages and getting services working again. Utility companies understand very well that their products and services are vital. The resiliency built into their distribution networks and the extensive resources that they keep poised to set things right are testaments to how seriously they take their missions.

Many IT organizations can justifiably argue that they already behave like utilities in terms of resiliency. They have round-the-clock network operations centers and help desks; they use virtualization technology to minimize the impact of storage failures. More and more are clustering their servers to shorten recovery times for critical applications. In these respects, they are indeed like utilities. Where they differ, however, is that they tend to lack service standardization and automated problem detection and analysis. Few restrict their users to specific server or storage configurations. Equally few are able to detect and recover from any but the simplest failures without human intervention. Since every application receives unique services and guarantees, the cost of resiliency is needlessly high, and the quality of service is needlessly low.

A Business

Even though utility companies deliver essential products and services, they operate as businesses. Users pay for what they use or what they have access to. Apart from a few socially motivated exceptions, such as subsidized services and guaranteed minimum coverage for the elderly, utility products and services are delivered on a pay-for-use basis.

The cost of utility commodities aside, one reason for a pay-for-use model is that utility products and services are taken for granted. If there weren't electricity bills to reckon with, why turn off the lights? If heating gas didn't cost money, why not turn the thermostat up and open the windows? If long-distance calls were free, why not tie up telephone circuits to play the latest popular CD to the nephew in Dubuque?

Computing has come to be regarded as a right of enterprise operational departments. Paying for the resources, however, is the IT department's problem. It is common for IT departments to spend money to meet operational needs and allocate cost across all users at the end of each fiscal year.

In the early days of enterprise computing, users were few, applications were static, and accountability was easy. Today, every employee has electronic mail and Web access (and relies on them to do her job), and business units feel free to request new Web sites, e-commerce portals, and other services. Accountability is both more essential and more difficult.

Business units have come to cherish the "I-want-it, I-get-it" IT service model, with no direct accountability for consumption. Even executives sometimes see IT accountability as inessential bureaucracy. Yet, it's hard to find a CIO who won't complain of ongoing budget pressure — stemming in part from the lack of motivation for users to moderate their demands.

Is IT Already a Utility?

If a utility is a business that provides essential services reliably to a broad consumer base, is IT a utility today? Consider the key implications of the definition:

- ***Is IT essential?*** Clearly it is. Today, few enterprises could survive without e-mail, databases, and Web access.
- ***Does IT provide a small set of services to a large user community?*** Yes and no. Electronic mail is available to most workers in most enterprises today. Services for most applications, however, are still "handcrafted," designed to meet unnecessarily unique requirements, with little or no standardization.
- ***Is IT delivered reliably?*** Yes and no. Most enterprises build resiliency into their most critical applications but don't standardize design and deployment techniques that could make resiliency available across the board. In part, this stems from the immaturity of the practice, but it is also a result of the complexity of information delivery. IT is far more complicated than electricity or water. Is the system down? Is response time deteriorating? Are there unexplainable errors (e.g., 404 Web access errors)? The number of possible failure modes makes delivering IT as a utility a formidable challenge.
- ***Is IT a business?*** Typically not. This is arguably the most difficult behavioral change in implementing an IT utility — the concept that users should pay for what they consume. Given the history (fluctuation from static chargeback to "free" computing to proportional allocation of cost), users are understandably skeptical of yet another change in accountability. But accountability may be the biggest benefit of utility computing. Only by accurately accounting for consumption can an enterprise balance the costs and benefits of information technology and make business decisions about "how much computing is enough."

Thus, while the conditions for utility delivery of IT services are present, IT is seldom delivered as a utility today, lacking the strictly defined service offerings, the reliability guarantees, and the accountability characteristic of conventional utility services.

What Utilities Aren't

In attempting to understand the essentials of the utility model, it is also instructive to consider what a utility *isn't*. Table 1-1 offers 12 examples of common services. Seven of the twelve are generally regarded as utilities — telephone, piped natural gas, electricity, water and sewer, cable television (CATV), satellite television (SATV), and broadband Internet access. The other five are not generally regarded as utilities — bottled natural gas, broadcast television, the United States Postal Service, newspaper delivery, and refuse collection.

	Telephone	Natural gas (piped)	Electricity	Water and sewer	CATV	SATV	Broadband Internet	Natural gas (bottled)	Broadcast television	U.S. Postal Service	Newspaper delivery	Refuse collection
Continuous availability	yes	yes	yes	yes	yes	yes	yes	no	yes	no	no	no
Available to anyone	yes	yes	yes	yes	yes	yes	yes	no	yes	yes	no	no
Measured consumption	yes	yes	yes	yes	yes	yes	yes	no	no	yes	no	no
Standard menu of services	yes	yes	yes	yes	yes	yes	yes	yes	yes	yes	yes	yes
Billing for usage or availability	yes	yes	yes	yes	yes	yes	yes	yes	no	no	no	Sometimes
Taken for granted by consumers	yes	yes	yes	yes	yes	yes	yes	no	yes	yes	yes	no
	← Utilities →							← Not utilities →				

Table 1-1: Distinguishing characteristics of services

Table 1-1 enumerates six key characteristics of enterprises. Services that are regarded as utilities generally exhibit all six of these characteristics, and those that do not meet all of the requirements are not utilities. For example, bottled gas service is certainly not available to everyone and is continuously available only to the extent that the user replenishes the supply. Television signals broadcast over the airwaves are not measured or charged back (indeed, the success of CATV and SATV is testimony to the adage that a free service is worth the price). As another example, readers who live in rural areas will recognize that refuse collection can involve user participation — far from the common notion of a utility.

Key Differentiators

Perhaps the most obvious differentiator between utilities and other companies is that a utility's services are delivered over a network that interconnects customers. Whether it's pipes or wires, a utility's always-there connection to users is what makes continuous service possible. Other companies tend to provide more intermittent services. But some non-utilities (e.g., broadcast television) do provide continuous service, so there must be further distinctions.

Utilities are ubiquitous within some defined service area, and therefore a second important characteristic of any utility is that it is available to anyone, provided they're located in that service area. For example, a natural gas utility provides a grid of pipes that deliver gas directly to consumers. If you aren't near those pipes, it's unlikely that the utility will be available to you, and you'll probably have to use bottled gas. However, if you are on or near the gas system you most likely have the service already. IT's service area is obviously the organization it serves, and the pipes are the enterprise network. If you're on the network, IT utility services are available to you.

A third important characteristic of utilities is standardization. Electric service is available in the United States at 110 and at 220 volts, period. Standardization of services makes it possible for electrical device manufacturers to build devices that work anywhere.

In some parts of the country, other companies tend to offer much more variety in their services. A call to the newspaper service or the trash collector may get the paper delivered to the back door or trash picked up on Tuesday rather than Monday. Many of today's IT projects share this characteristic — each application's requirements are met without regard for what is offered elsewhere in the data center. This lack of standardization ultimately ripples into operational complexity and a lower-than-necessary quality of service.

The fourth common characteristic of utilities is that they are able to monitor use of their services. Electricity, gas, and water charges are all based on consumption. Local telephone service rates (in the United States) are generally based on a fixed fee, while long-distance rates are connection time-based, but in both cases, providers can track usage down to the second. Even cable television, which is almost always flat fee-based, is able to provide "pay-per-view" offerings. All utilities can capture usage information; many other companies do not have this ability.

Fifth, utilities bill their customers regularly for what they use. Whether it's water, electricity, or cable TV, users pay for services in a way that relates to consumption. In contrast, other companies tend to use either a retail sale model (ad hoc purchases, as with bottled gas) or a taxation model (possibly unrelated to consumption). Retail models make it difficult to forecast demand and therefore to provide consistent service. Taxation with periodic chargeback, which is how much of IT operates today, makes accountability nearly impossible.

Last but far from least, the sixth primary characteristic of a utility is that it is taken for granted by the consumers. Our earlier example of the blackouts in New York illustrate this point most vividly: Because the service is assumed to be "on" at all times, when it isn't there is widespread disruption. Any interruption in phone service, power, and water supply will result in a drastic suspension of normal routine. Instead, the affected citizens mobilize an onerous and hopefully temporary emergency procedure whose primary concern is basic survival. IT fits this model already. Without the network, e-mail, computer documents, and enterprise applications, the company or organization simply stops until service can be restored. The user community takes IT services for granted. Unfortunately, thanks largely to the relative unreliability of vendor equipment and software, users take outages — and business interruption — for granted as well.

Utilities and Governments

For most enterprises, IT is essential — there's no enterprise without it. Recognizing its importance, many enterprises provide information services to business lines and operational departments with only a cursory insight into cost. This is similar to the model of government taxation used to fund services like police, fire protection, and so forth. In some enterprises, IT resembles these government services, especially their financial model: Operational expenses are part of the enterprise (government) budget; departments (taxpayers) pay allocations (assessments) that are loosely related to consumption if at all.

Transforming IT into a utility may be considered analogous to privatization of a government service. The hallmark of successful privatization is a service that works better and costs less than before privatization.

Utilities and Quality of Service

Because the services that they provide are essential, utilities are often required by law to monitor them. Monitoring goes beyond usage tracking — it implies failure alerts, remote diagnosis, and centrally managed (and where possible automated) repair. Some utilities are more sophisticated than others (for example, the cable television companies are very good at catching people who steal their service), but some level of monitoring is universal. Ironically, the utilities with the least sophisticated monitoring capabilities (e.g., water, municipal gas) tend to be the most reliable. Conversely, less reliable services, such as broadband Internet, generally have very sophisticated tools for alerting, remote diagnosis, and centralized repair and management.

The sophistication of monitoring is motivated by the complexity of a service; it's much harder to diagnose a slow DSL link than a leaking water main. The lesson for utility computing is that success depends on tools that enable the kind of service that users expect from their utilities.

This discussion gives a basis for concisely stating a working definition of a utility:

> utility *n* : A business that provides a standardized menu of essential services reliably enough that they can be taken for granted by users. Utilities provide their services over continuously available monitored connections. A utility finances itself by billing users in a way that reflects the value or cost of providing the service consumed.

The chapters that follow describe how utility computing can streamline the delivery of enterprise information services using this utility delivery model.

Chapter Summary

- A utility is a business that provides a small set of standardized essential services to a large user community reliably enough that they can be taken for granted.
- Information technology is clearly essential to enterprises, but today it is often not provided according to a utility model. IT services are often not standardized, have variable reliability, and are seldom tracked in sufficient detail for reasonable chargeback.
- Utilities' standard menu of products and services are continuously available to anyone in the potential user community. They are taken for granted by users, and their consumption or availability is measured and charged back to users.
- Companies that are not regarded as utilities fail to fulfill one of these criteria.
- The ability to monitor service usage and bill for it is key to the utility model of product and service delivery. Accountability is a key differentiator between an IT utility and a conventional IT delivery organization.

CHAPTER 2

Why Utility Computing

"Order is Heaven's first law."

— Alexander Pope

In this chapter...

- How the key characteristics of utilities lead to benefits
- How the benefits and limitations of utility-style operation apply to information technology
- Decision factors in adopting utility computing

Chapter 1 discusses the utility concept. This chapter explains why certain products and services can be delivered so effectively by the utility model and the characteristics those products and services share with information technology.

Benefits of Utility-Style Operation

Utilities offer significant benefits to both users and their providers. These benefits derive in large part from the four fundamental properties of utilities enumerated in Chapter 1:

- The scale on which they operate
- The narrow range of their service offerings
- The reliability that they deliver
- The financial model they adhere to

The sections that follow discuss these properties of utilities, the benefits they convey, and their application to the delivery of information technology services.

Scale

With utilities, bigger is better. The largest serve tens of millions of users. In part, the number of potential users is what justifies the cost of a utility's distribution network.

Once a utility's distribution network is in place, it becomes an advantage. Assuming that it has adequate coverage and access points, the network makes it possible to serve new users and deliver additional services at minimal incremental cost.

The benefits of large-scale operation go beyond the network. With many users sharing the cost, more and better services can be provided. One thousand consumers might not justify (be able to afford) an advanced purification plant, but 100,000 probably could. With enough users sharing the cost, an electric company can upgrade its generators to provide cleaner, more reliable power. A larger user base also justifies more sophisticated diagnostic equipment to solve unexpected problems quickly.

Moreover, people and organizations become more proficient at doing things that they do often. A cable TV company that frequently repairs damage from lightning strikes or digging accidents becomes good at making those repairs — so good, in fact, that it might upgrade equipment or change operating procedures to help reduce accidents.

IT can also benefit from large-scale operation. For example, enterprise networks make it easy to deliver new information services throughout an organization. Similarly, consolidating storage and servers improves security and environmental control (and therefore reliability) and makes more professional management possible.

IT organizations have long recognized the benefit of specialized roles. Every data center has network, database, and system administrators, as well as help desk technicians, who are all good at what they do because they do it a lot. Specialization is most feasible in environments where there is enough work to justify specialists — again, bigger leads to better.

Range of Services

Utility users choose from small menus of products and services. Because their products are few, utilities usually understand them very well — from delivery cost to maintenance and upgrade to demand forecasting.

Because their service offerings are simple, utilities can predict and prepare for demand. Despite occasional anecdotes of utility companies taking months to install new services, they are generally able to cope with fluctuations in demand. Indeed, the fact that breakdowns in utility service are so memorable is evidence of the proposition that with utilities, things usually "just work."

Reliability

With only a few products to attend to, utilities can tune them and their delivery networks to a high degree of reliability. Intimate product knowledge leads to efficient operating procedures, as well as training and auditing to ensure adherence. Ticketing, work order, and dispatch systems track every network modification and service change, ensuring that the users' service requests don't get "lost."

The utility model should also improve IT reliability. A narrow range of services can be "packaged" for fast, reliable deployment. Streamlining services means fewer components to forecast and stock, and therefore faster response to both planned and unanticipated needs. Problems can be resolved faster because fewer situations that support staff "have never seen before" arise.

Financial Model

Part of utilities' knowledge of their products is understanding and controlling cost. Today, most IT organizations don't have the detailed cost models typical of utilities. But even without sophisticated models, the cost of basic IT services should be easily calculable and used to control IT costs. Most organizations should be able to estimate the cost of common services, such as implementing a new database or making nightly backups, using information that could be available to them today.

Utilities are typically profitable, even though in many cases the government regulates their prices. Utilities are often prevented from raising prices by regulation or other external factors, so, in many cases, the only way that they can increase profits is to cut costs. IT departments aren't exactly expected to generate profits, but detailed knowledge and strong cost controls are still beneficial. Lower unit cost means that more or better service can be provided with a given budget. Alternatively, a smaller IT expense line improves profitability or, for nonprofit enterprises, reduces the cost of operations.

Roles and Communications

Because of their scale, their need for efficient operation, and the maturity of their businesses, utility companies are necessarily highly specialized along functional lines. Engineering, operations, customer service, billing, etc., are all separate departments.

A corollary of well-defined functional roles is well-defined interfaces and lines of communication between functions. People are sometimes surprised to discover that CATV and telephone installers have had no contact with order takers, and yet they know exactly what's expected of them. Over time, utilities have learned exactly what must be communicated between functions and how best to communicate it.

By contrast, a typical IT organization has a help desk for first-level customer support, but beyond that, engineering, operations, provisioning, escalation, monitoring, and recovery roles tend to overlap. Few IT organizations have accounting or billing specialists. For utility computing to succeed, IT vendors must help enterprises automate data center operations. Automation, particularly of data center workflow, will facilitate role-based operations for greater efficiency and better quality of service.

Successful utilities manage changes in their delivery networks with little or no user impact. Telephone companies introduce new features like caller ID and three-way calling with no noticeable interruption in service. Utilities' configuration management procedures are typically highly evolved and rigorously enforced. Nothing is done without an authorized work order, countersigned by affected parties.

Strict control over configuration changes is critical for an IT utility. Today, most IT organizations exercise change control over their networks, systems, and applications. Those that enforce it (alas, not all do) tend to have more reliable systems and networks. A few have extended change control to include operations and user relationship management, but the well-defined roles and relationships that characterize utilities remain exceptional in IT organizations.

Capacity and Performance Management

Because their distribution networks are flexible, electric companies can quickly and seamlessly increase supply to areas that are experiencing unusually high demand.[3] They can do this because they have detailed real-time information about where consumption is occurring. Some reconfiguration operations are even automatic.

IT organizations build flexibility into their infrastructures but generally lack the detailed real-time performance information that would allow them to dynamically reallocate resources to meet changing demand. A new generation of IT management tools (that includes VERITAS CommandCentral™ Service software) is emerging. These tools not only detect deteriorating performance, but they can automatically reallocate resources to limit the impact of slowdowns. They improve IT performance management in two ways:

- They provide real-time information in enough detail to support meaningful decisions about resource reallocation.
- In some cases they can automate the decision making, reducing the routine administrative attention required to keep a data center running smoothly.

Limitations of the Utility Model

A methodology such as the utility model imposes discipline on the systems that it governs, sometimes forcing users to abandon familiar ways of doing things in favor of new mechanisms that may appear to be overly rigid and impose higher overhead. The sections that follow examine the inherent rigidity and overhead of utility computing.

Rigidity

While most utilities can respond quickly to changes in demand, they are slow to make significant changes in their services or offer new ones. Indeed, the utility model's success is due in part to the extensive planning that precedes each new service introduction. While competitive pressures have made some utilities much more agile of late (for example, the battle between telecommunication providers and CATV companies), it remains difficult for a utility to radically change its service offering.

By adopting the utility model, an IT organization necessarily makes itself more rigid and resistant to fundamental change. Equipment,

3. Notwithstanding the blackout in the northeastern United States in August of 2003.

deployment processes, and service offerings all become standardized. But occasionally, standard offerings fail to meet a user's needs, and a custom solution is legitimately required.

In practice, it may be impossible for an IT organization to operate as a pure utility. The rate of change and variety of applications in IT are both much greater than with traditional utilities. For example, a decade ago, there was effectively no Internet. As recently as five years ago, it was primarily a source for static information. Today, the Internet carries a huge amount of commerce.[4] This rapid growth has driven major changes in IT. For example, a typical enterprise:

- Created Web information services (1993)
- Implemented business-to-consumer access portals (1996)
- Secured its portals against intrusion (1997)
- Integrated its portals into mainstream corporate information processing (1998)
- Added business-to-business capabilities (1999)
- Made the Internet its principal conduit for doing business (2001)
- Secured network against a rash of new worms and viruses (2003)

With the exception of mobile communications, it is difficult to think of a service environment that has undergone so much change so quickly. If this pace continues, it may never be possible for IT organizations to behave completely as utilities. CIOs should not regard support for an occasional customized service as failure, as long as most of their data centers operate according to a utility model.

Overhead

Utilities have made enormous investments in specialized personnel and equipment, from custom hardware like elevated platform trucks ("cherry-pickers") to their own fire departments. Fortunately, much of the special equipment that an IT utility needs is actually software. Today, many IT organizations already have some of the necessary tools, like network analyzers and diagnostics, in place. Some are equipped with ticketing and workflow software as well. More sophisticated tools now becoming available enhance IT organizations' ability to operate as

4. The Securities Industry Association says that 34 percent of traders who traded equities in 2001 used the Internet.

utilities with features like automated server and storage provisioning, diagnosis and repair, event handling, cost accounting, and service level tracking. Figure 2-1 is an event handling display from one such tool — VERITAS CommandCentral Service.

While a transition to utility computing will require investments, the investments will not be nearly as large as those for a traditional utility. Moreover, some of the overhead elements may already be in place. Planning and execution are the keys to utility computing success, not massive capital outlay.

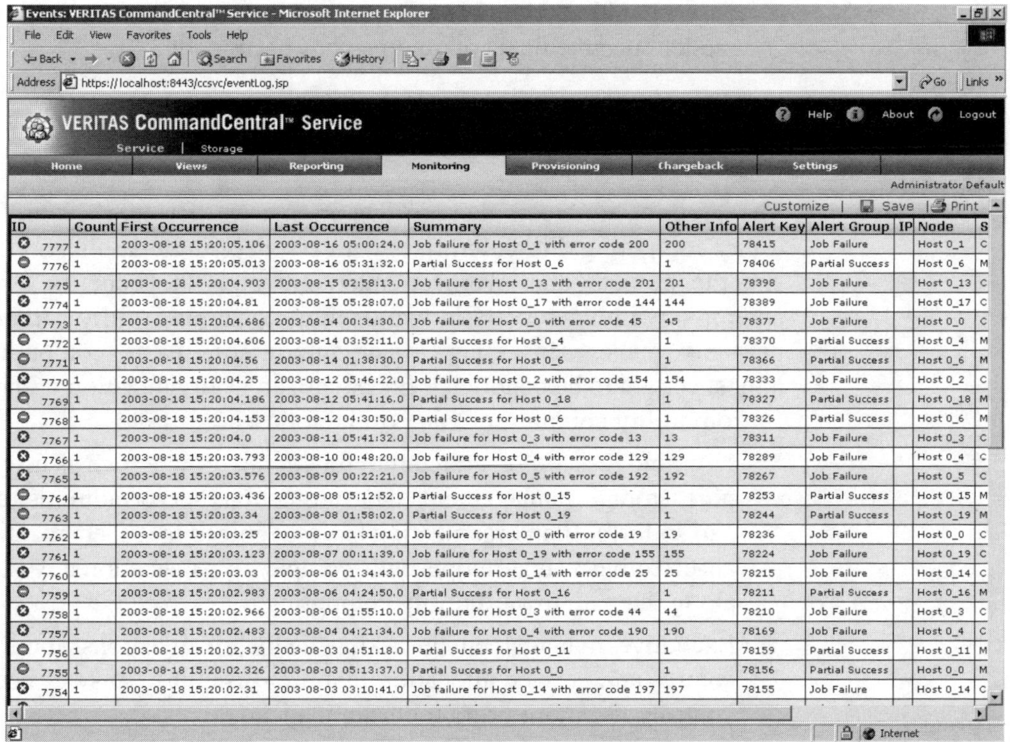

ID	Count	First Occurrence	Last Occurrence	Summary	Other Info	Alert Key	Alert Group	IP	Node	S
7777	1	2003-08-18 15:20:05.106	2003-08-16 05:00:24.0	Job failure for Host 0_1 with error code 200	200	78415	Job Failure		Host 0_1	C
7776	1	2003-08-18 15:20:05.013	2003-08-16 05:31:32.0	Partial Success for Host 0_6	1	78406	Partial Success		Host 0_6	M
7775	1	2003-08-18 15:20:04.903	2003-08-15 02:58:13.0	Job failure for Host 0_13 with error code 201	201	78398	Job Failure		Host 0_13	C
7774	1	2003-08-18 15:20:04.81	2003-08-15 05:28:07.0	Job failure for Host 0_17 with error code 144	144	78389	Job Failure		Host 0_17	C
7773	1	2003-08-18 15:20:04.686	2003-08-14 00:34:30.0	Job failure for Host 0_0 with error code 45	45	78377	Job Failure		Host 0_0	C
7772	1	2003-08-18 15:20:04.606	2003-08-14 03:52:11.0	Partial Success for Host 0_4	1	78370	Partial Success		Host 0_4	M
7771	1	2003-08-18 15:20:04.56	2003-08-14 01:38:30.0	Partial Success for Host 0_6	1	78366	Partial Success		Host 0_6	M
7770	1	2003-08-18 15:20:04.25	2003-08-12 05:46:22.0	Job failure for Host 0_2 with error code 154	154	78333	Job Failure		Host 0_2	C
7769	1	2003-08-18 15:20:04.186	2003-08-12 05:41:16.0	Partial Success for Host 0_18	1	78327	Partial Success		Host 0_18	M
7768	1	2003-08-18 15:20:04.153	2003-08-12 04:30:50.0	Partial Success for Host 0_6	1	78326	Partial Success		Host 0_6	M
7767	1	2003-08-18 15:20:04.0	2003-08-11 05:41:32.0	Job failure for Host 0_3 with error code 13	13	78311	Job Failure		Host 0_3	C
7766	1	2003-08-18 15:20:03.793	2003-08-10 00:48:20.0	Job failure for Host 0_4 with error code 129	129	78289	Job Failure		Host 0_4	C
7765	1	2003-08-18 15:20:03.576	2003-08-09 00:22:21.0	Job failure for Host 0_5 with error code 192	192	78267	Job Failure		Host 0_5	C
7764	1	2003-08-18 15:20:03.436	2003-08-08 05:12:52.0	Partial Success for Host 0_15	1	78253	Partial Success		Host 0_15	M
7763	1	2003-08-18 15:20:03.34	2003-08-08 01:58:02.0	Partial Success for Host 0_19	1	78244	Partial Success		Host 0_19	M
7762	1	2003-08-18 15:20:03.25	2003-08-07 01:31:01.0	Job failure for Host 0_0 with error code 19	19	78236	Job Failure		Host 0_0	C
7761	1	2003-08-18 15:20:03.123	2003-08-07 00:11:39.0	Job failure for Host 0_19 with error code 155	155	78224	Job Failure		Host 0_19	C
7760	1	2003-08-18 15:20:03.03	2003-08-06 01:34:43.0	Job failure for Host 0_14 with error code 25	25	78215	Job Failure		Host 0_14	C
7759	1	2003-08-18 15:20:02.983	2003-08-06 04:24:50.0	Partial Success for Host 0_16	1	78211	Partial Success		Host 0_16	M
7758	1	2003-08-18 15:20:02.966	2003-08-06 01:55:10.0	Job failure for Host 0_3 with error code 44	44	78210	Job Failure		Host 0_3	C
7757	1	2003-08-18 15:20:02.483	2003-08-04 04:21:34.0	Job failure for Host 0_4 with error code 190	190	78169	Job Failure		Host 0_4	C
7756	1	2003-08-18 15:20:02.373	2003-08-03 04:51:18.0	Partial Success for Host 0_11	1	78159	Partial Success		Host 0_11	M
7755	1	2003-08-18 15:20:02.326	2003-08-03 05:13:37.0	Partial Success for Host 0_0	1	78156	Partial Success		Host 0_0	M
7754	1	2003-08-18 15:20:02.31	2003-08-03 03:10:41.0	Job failure for Host 0_14 with error code 197	197	78155	Job Failure		Host 0_14	C

Figure 2-1: An automated event handler (VERITAS CommandCentral Service)

Making the IT Utility Decision

Utility computing offers advantages (better quality of service, faster deployment, and above all, lower administrative cost) and has certain limitations (rigidity and overhead). Like most business decisions, an IT utility choice depends on whether the benefits outweigh the limitations. The two key questions for IT organizations are:

- Should an IT organization adopt the utility computing model for its information technology?
- How should an enterprise go about adopting the utility computing model once the decision to do so has been made?

Decision Factors

The larger or more complex an IT operation, the greater the benefits of utility computing. For enterprises with 10 or so single-application servers, the process and overhead may outweigh the benefits. For an enterprise with 25 servers in two or more locations, utility computing probably makes sense. For larger enterprises, utility computing is almost certain to be beneficial. In general, an IT organization will benefit from utility computing if any of the following is true:

- IT employees are separated into functional groups such as user support, storage management, data protection, server administration, and so forth. If an organization has recognized that specialization is an effective way to cope with complexity, it has already started along the path toward utility computing.
- Executive management is asking awkward questions about cost control and service allocation that are difficult to answer because controls and monitoring tools are inadequate.
- Executive management wants operating units to be individually responsible for their IT costs (this allocation model is common for items like real estate and telephone service), but there is no feasible way to determine and allocate them.

Any of these factors by itself may indicate that an organization is ready for utility computing. Two of them together send a strong signal that utility computing should be considered. If all three are true, the organization should probably be evaluating utility computing formally as Chapter 5 describes.

There are even some information technology-oriented enterprises that have adopted utility computing for their own operations and used the experience gained to launch businesses to help other enterprises move their IT operations to the utility model.

Getting Started

As with any significant enterprisewide change, the success of utility computing depends heavily on executive support. Operating departments accustomed to getting exactly what they want the way they want it can be expected to resist the standardization of the utility model. Without executive support, the procedural changes can result in interdepartmental friction, increasing the cost and duration of the transition, and endangering its success.

Once an executive decision to adopt utility computing has been made, implementation is the responsibility of the IT organization. It is a rare CIO who can change an IT organization so radically all at once. Like any major undertaking, a transition to utility computing should be thoroughly planned with clear targets (services to be provided), detailed requirements, and a stepwise implementation plan. Chapter 5 discusses evaluation of the utility concept and planning the transition. Chapter 6 describes the execution of a transition to utility computing.

Chapter Summary

- Each of the four fundamental characteristics of utilities — their scale of operation, the narrow range of services, the reliability of their infrastructures, and their accountability models — has benefits for users and operators. For the most part, these benefits also apply to information technology infrastructures operating on utility principles.
- Also inherent in the utility model is a clear definition of organizational responsibilities and the interfaces between them. For the most part, these clear distinctions do not exist in IT organizations today, but they are a required procedural change if utility computing is to succeed.
- The utility model does impose some rigidity (for example, on service offerings) and suffers from a certain inherent overhead (for

formal service request and infrastructure change tracking). In the case of IT, the apparent rigidity can actually be beneficial to users as well as operators, and the overhead is minor and has, in some cases, already sunk cost.

- The benefits of utility computing are directly proportional to the size of the enterprise IT operation — larger organizations benefit to a greater extent. Nevertheless, the benefits may not be obvious to the (all-important) users. Therefore, a decision to adopt the IT utility model should only be undertaken with strong executive-level support that is communicated clearly throughout the enterprise.

CHAPTER 3

A Day in the Life of a Utility

"The past is ignorant of the present. Be careful in taking its advice."

— Mason Cooley

In this chapter...

- Day-to-day activities in a utility company
- Creation, deployment, operation, accounting, and maintenance of utility services
- Application of utility processes to information technology delivery

An IT organization performs many of the same tasks as a utility company. Both must:

- Create service offerings
- Allocate resources to provide services
- Monitor operations
- Track service costs and the resultant value
- Provide access to services
- Handle user complaints
- Maintain the service infrastructure and delivery network

Most data centers aren't as rigorous about standardizing their services as a utility. The opportunity for cost reduction and improved service quality lies in making enterprise IT more utility-like in the following areas:

- Standardized services
- Automated provisioning
- Dynamic adjustment of the delivery network to meet changing demands
- Strict accounting for cost and consumption

To appreciate how this might work, it is useful to consider day-to-day life in a utility (again comparing conditions in a classic utility with those typically found in information technology). Figure 3-1 illustrates a typical utility workflow.

As Figure 3-1 suggests, a utility *creates* services and *deploys* them (using its delivery network). It *operates* the network and the resource infrastructure behind it and *accounts* for the cost of its services, generating bills based on user consumption. The following sections analyze these functions in more detail and apply the analyses to IT environments.

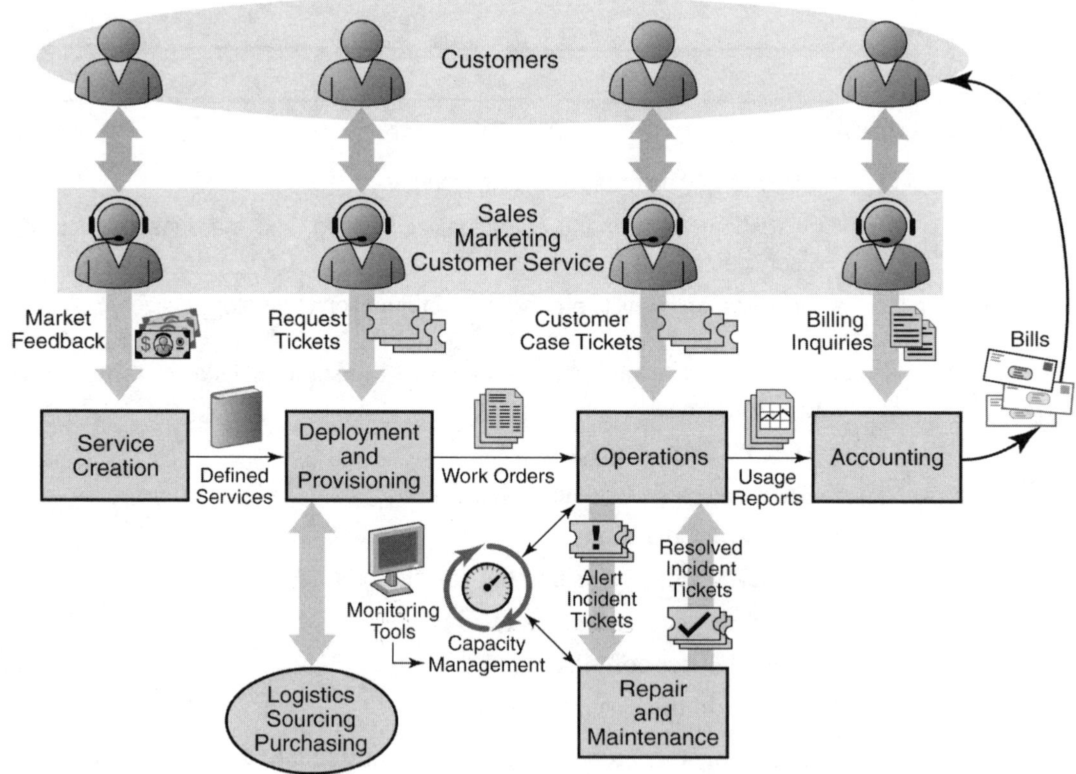

Figure 3-1: Workflow in a typical utility

Service Creation

A utility must clearly define the services that it will offer so that they can be packaged for efficient delivery. Service offerings should be based on the most thorough market research that can be done. Service creation teams should base their definitions on documented user requirements.

Information technology services are typically defined by engineering or development teams with guidance from other parts of the enterprise. When a newly defined service is deployed, responsibility passes to an operating or administrative team. Developers may be the last line of support but are usually not otherwise involved in day-to-day operations.

IT services are a mixture of unique and standard elements — hardware, software, procedures, and staff. A service definition developed by an IT utility might include the following elements:

- ***Content specification***. The function the service will perform (e.g., online storage, backup, server capacity), including performance, availability, downtime, recovery time, lead time, disaster recovery, and pricing parameters.
- ***Operations specification***. Operating procedures, maintenance, and call escalation handling. Specifications for tools and supplies.
- ***Facility specification***. Incremental hardware, software, physical space, network access, and other facilities. Initial requirements and projected growth. Vendor selection and planning for initial and ongoing purchases.
- ***Staff specification***. Staffing requirements during development, deployment, and ongoing operation and maintenance.
- ***Schedule***. Milestones for development and deployment, including design completion, development completion, equipment delivery and setup, testing, and administrative assignment and training.
- ***Cost and pricing analysis***. Cost of creation, ongoing routine operation, overhead, maintenance, and upgrade. Determination of charging algorithms and billing procedures.

An IT service definition should be a change-controlled document, because it is both the work product of the developers and the vehicle for communicating the nature of the service to the operations team. The service definition should be distributed to key people throughout the enterprise, and training should be provided.

An IT utility service definition should include a *service-level agreement* (SLA) template that defines the bounds of the service (e.g., how few and how many gigabytes of premium storage can be contracted, how short a backup time per gigabyte can be contracted, and so forth). Developers define SLA parameters for a service, and the customer service team negotiates user agreements within the bounds of those parameters. SLA parameters make *tiered services* (functionally equivalent services delivered at different performance and availability levels for different costs) possible.

Deployment and Provisioning

Once defined, an IT service must be deployed. Deployment includes purchase and installation of resources (e.g., RAID systems for an online storage service) and any necessary incremental infrastructure (e.g., additional switches for the storage network), as well as drafting operating procedures and training operators, administrators, and service staff. Deployment also includes secondary tasks:

- Asset tracking (recording the disposition of all equipment allocated to the service in an operations database)
- Enabling monitoring
- Rehearsing incident management procedures
- Adding appropriate individuals to a *rota* (a prioritized list of people who should be contacted in the event of an incident)

Provisioning

Once equipment, infrastructure, and trained staff are in place, the service can be delivered to users. In an IT utility, *provisioning*[5] is initiated by a customer service request, represented as a work order in a *workflow* or *ticketing system*. A sophisticated workflow system will include approvals for purchasing, receiving, and installing equipment, as well as a user acceptance signoff indicating agreement that service has begun. Figure 3-2 shows a screen display from the VERITAS CommandCentral Service workflow management system.

5. The term *provisioning* has multiple meanings in information technology. It is used here to mean "providing a service to a customer." In other contexts, it is used to mean "deploying a service" (as described in this section) and "adding resources to a service."

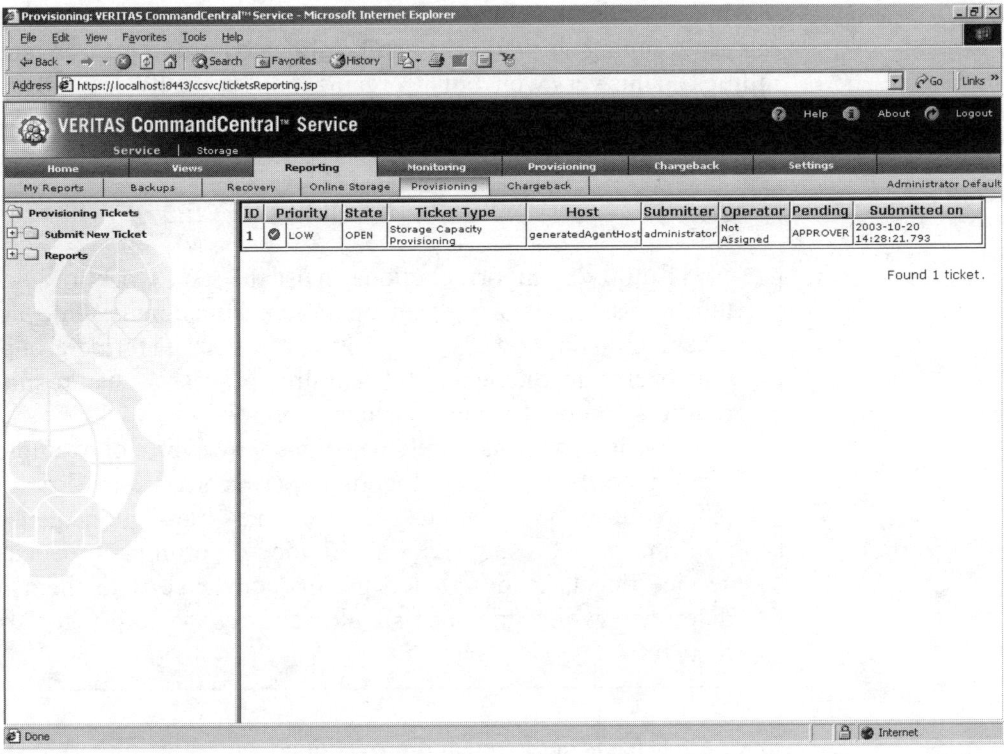

Figure 3-2: A workflow management system (VERITAS CommandCentral Service)

There are two components to IT service provisioning, both of which are equally critical to successful deployment:

- ***Central provisioning***. Making required configuration changes to the infrastructure (e.g., adding user accounts)
- ***Field provisioning***. Delivering and installing any required equipment and software at the user site (e.g., database or backup client installation)

Once a service has been provisioned and tested, delivery begins.

Some IT components are capable of *automated provisioning*, dynamically increasing or decreasing the amount of resource allocated to a given user within preauthorized limits without human intervention. Typically, automated provisioning is used to modify the level of service to existing users (e.g., the amount of storage allocated to a database) rather than to add new ones.

It is essential to collect complete and accurate user information during provisioning so that costs can be allocated properly. Conventional utilities do this very well, but IT organizations typically do not. Business alignment requires accurate cost accounting.

A Note on Ticketing Systems

An IT utility's support function can use the same workflow system as its provisioning and operations functions. While not essential, a single workflow system can help integrate groups that exchange incidents and simplify processes that require multiple approvals, such as change control.

Workflow systems should be simple, however. For example, making notification and accepting approvals via e-mail rather than requiring login and use of specialized transactions generally improves responsiveness. Some IT utilities broadcast service tickets to designated groups and leave it to them to determine which member should take responsibility for the incident.

Once a service is deployed and provisioned, ongoing delivery responsibility moves to the operations function. Especially in larger IT utilities, the handoff should be formal (perhaps utilizing the workflow system) to ensure that provisioning is complete and SLAs are clearly understood by all parties.

Operations

The goal of any utility service is flawless delivery, but even the best-designed services experience occasional faults, so operations staff must be prepared to deal with them. Traditional utilities operate elaborate custom-designed operations centers. A large utility's operations center might seat dozens of specialists and use colorful status displays as big as movie screens. A few large IT organizations have similar centers, but most use desktop workstations and personal computers. IT utility operations centers do not inherently require elaborate facilities.

Today, tools are available to automate much of the work of an IT utility operations center. There are automated monitoring systems that sense anomalies (e.g., steadily increasing response times) and send *alerts* to *event consoles* (computers that collect, filter, correlate, and display events from throughout the network). For events that require attention, operations specialists create *incidents* (detailed ongoing records of events) in ticketing systems that track each incident through resolution. Typically, operations staffs themselves deal with the most common problems; obscure or complex problems are escalated to specialists. A rota defines the order in which specialists are consulted.

Fully automated IT utility operations centers can also collect and record the data required to measure actual performance against SLAs. From an availability standpoint, if asset and user data is acquired during deployment and provisioning, it is possible to automatically determine which users are affected by a given outage.

Accounting

Accounting (keeping detailed records of the amount of resources consumed by users) is fundamental to the business side of utility operation. One of the greatest potential benefits of the IT utility concept (and one of the most fundamental behavioral changes for enterprises) is the detailed knowledge that ultimately enables IT costs to be aligned with business benefits.

In a mature utility, execution of a work order creates records that indicate which resources a user may consume and triggers automatic collection of data about actual consumption. Thereafter, resource utilization, performance against SLA, and other billing information are recorded automatically and forwarded to the accounting function, which generates management reports and possibly bills.

Today, most IT departments do not directly charge users for service, and therefore they do not typically track individual user consumption. Chargeback for information services is a controversial topic in many enterprises, with important business ramifications outside the sphere of IT. But even without direct chargeback, business unit IT utilization data is a powerful management tool that can improve capacity planning and help ensure that each business unit and application receives IT resources commensurate with its importance to the enterprise.

Ongoing User Service

One of the most important functions in a utility is customer service, the ongoing direct link to users. Users register complaints by telephone, by electronic or paper mail, in person, and even through third parties such as governmental or regulatory bodies. A utility must be prepared to handle complaints from all of these sources.

Ongoing user service is one way in which many IT organizations do operate like utilities today. Complaint handling generally begins with a dedicated front-line support staff (a help desk) whose primary responsibility is to receive complaints, collect as much information as possible, and log incidents in an automated tracking system. This staff usually handles routine issues itself (e.g., forgotten passwords or locked or deleted files); more complex problems are delivered to the correct level in the support rota for resolution (up to and including engineering for the most complex issues). With a sophisticated ticketing system, delivery and tracking of incidents can be automatic. Typically, the first-line support staff is responsible for tracking all open incidents, no matter who handles them, and ensuring timely resolution.

Maintenance and Repair

A utility discovers problems through internal alerts reported to operations and through user complaints to the customer service department. In both cases, genuine failures are resolved by the maintenance and repair function.

Traditional utilities have specialist teams for each of their major infrastructure and resource elements. For example, electricity companies have specialists for generators, transmission lines, end-user facilities, etc. These specialists are generally part of the operations department and responsible for ongoing infrastructure operation, including preventive maintenance.

Issues that aren't resolved by first-level support are escalated to these specialists according to their positions in the rota. Clearly, specialists must have access to the ticketing system, event consoles, and customer service systems for progress tracking.

Similar protocols can be found in most IT organizations, the biggest difference being that service developers are often also responsible for resolving complex operational problems. Playing multiple roles is appropriate in smaller enterprises or data centers that run only a few applications, but should be reviewed periodically as an IT organization grows and operations begin to migrate toward the utility model.

Chapter Summary

- Each service that a utility offers must be created, deployed, operated (delivered to users on an ongoing basis), accounted for, and maintained.
- Creation of a utility service includes defining the offering, the delivery infrastructure, and the mechanisms for servicing users, accounting and billing, and maintaining the infrastructure.
- For true utility-style operation, service usage must be monitored to detect problems and record utilization data for accounting purposes.
- Utilities' service accounting requires information from the deployment function (capital expense and installation cost data), provisioning (user and SLA information), and operations (utilization and performance against SLA).
- Utilities typically provide tiers of service to their users. Help desk specialists field calls, track incidents, and resolve simple issues. More complex issues are routed to more technically oriented staff. Typically, IT organization support functions are not as functionally organized as those of other utilities. IT service developers are often responsible for ongoing remedial support.
- Utilities' maintenance and repair organizations are typically tiered as well. Traditional utilities' maintenance organizations invariably have dedicated technical specialists at several levels. Again, IT organizations tend not to have such precisely defined specializations for maintenance and repair.

CHAPTER 4

Is Utility Computing Really New?

"I think there is a world market for maybe five computers."

— Thomas Watson (1874-1956), Chairman of IBM, 1943

In this chapter...

- The roots of utility computing
- Important technological developments that have re-enabled utility computing
- Thoughts on the future of utility computing

Arguably, utility computing is the original form of computing. The high cost of early mainframe computers made them inherently enterprise resources. The computer (usually singular) was shared out of fiscal necessity. The technology of the time also encouraged utility-style operation. Ordinary people did not interact with computers; they prepared "jobs" on punched cards, which they submitted to specialists, who in turn queued them for execution in an order determined by the user's importance. As jobs completed, printed results would be returned to their submitters.

During the mainframe era, it was common for IT departments to charge users for the system resources that they consumed. Charges would be based on resources used, with rates reflecting relative priority and other factors such as time of day. In effect, a user's willingness to pay would determine the priority (level of service).

In the mainframe era, chargeback was a fiscal necessity because of the high cost of computing; it was just too expensive for detailed cost accounting to be ignored. Moreover, cost accounting was technically easy. A user's job would run on one computer, whose utilization could be measured. Data was stored typically on removable "disk packs," each allocated to a single application. Printers and other resources were concentrated in one place, and their use was easily associated with jobs.

Thus, computing in the mainframe era operated very much as a utility. Services were limited, delivery was centralized, and there was strict accounting and billing. The utility was an exclusive one, however. Because of the cost, computing was only available to large corporations, government agencies, and academic institutions. Individual departments, small users, and the general public had no access.

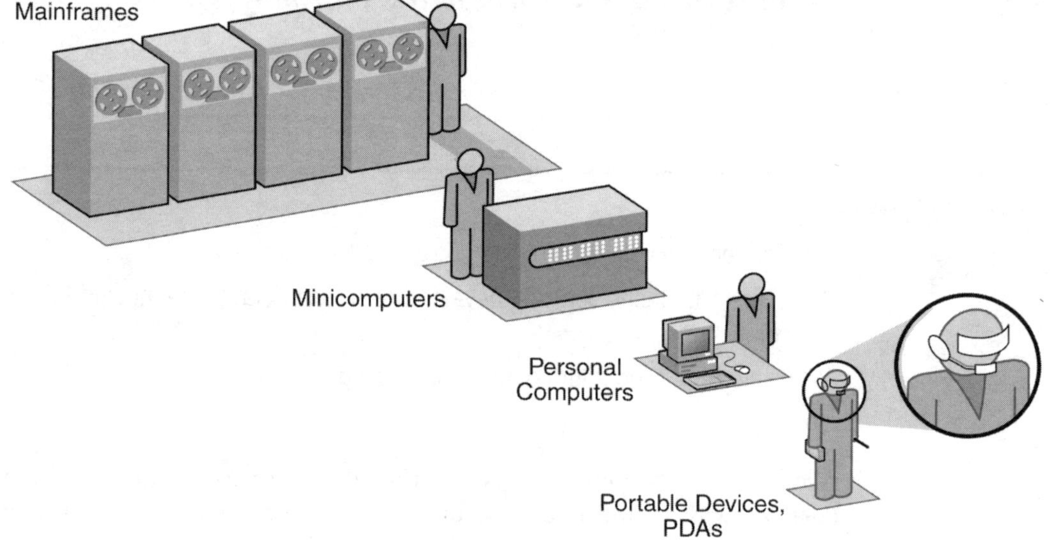

Figure 4-1: The evolution of enterprise computing

Open Systems and the Utility Model

During the 1960s and 1970s, technology advances steadily delivered smaller and less expensive computers. In the 1980s, UNIX-based open systems matured, making administrative skills transferable. Computer usage increased accordingly, and servers dedicated to individual enterprise functions like order processing and inventory control became common, even in small enterprises.

Paradoxically, the commoditization of computing diminished the utility delivery model, as single-purpose, low-cost computers transformed computing from a shared service into a departmental expense item. Computing went from being delivered by a central IT department to being delivered to each department by departmentally owned computers. Computing came to be treated as departmental capital outlay rather than as an ongoing expense shared across the enterprise.

Personal Computers

In the 1980s, computing became available directly to consumers, starting with kits, and was followed closely by complete self-contained personal computers. Over the course of the decade, prices plummeted and the number of users and applications rose correspondingly. Individuals could afford computers that could do things they considered useful — writing letters, keeping budgets, playing games, and exchanging electronic mail. It didn't take long for these low-cost devices to find their way back into the enterprise, supplanting "dumb" terminals connected to large mainframe servers.

The usefulness of a personal computer increases with its processing power. Today's personal computers are as powerful as the supercomputers of 1990 and easily capable of running applications that once required large data centers. Computing power has effectively become a commodity — low in cost and deliverable in interchangeable units by a variety of vendors.

But low-cost processing by itself would not be sufficient to engender utility computing; a distribution network was also required. The utility computing concept described in preceding chapters would not be possible without a parallel development in information technology — Ethernet and the pervasive networking that resulted.

Connectivity: The Great Enabler

From the earliest days of computing, it was clear that interconnecting computers would dramatically increase their usefulness. The defense establishment acted on this belief early — in the 1960s, the RAND Corporation sought ways for the United States to maintain control of its missiles and defense systems after a nuclear attack. The research led to the development of packet-switching network protocols with very flexible routing and a high degree of robustness.

Peer Networks

The United States government's Advanced Research Projects Agency (ARPA) used packet-switching technology to construct the peer-based ARPAnet. The ARPAnet initially linked universities; later it was extended to include defense contractors. Although computers had been interconnected before, the ARPAnet was the first one designed for peer relationships among computers — instead of one master computer issuing commands to slaves, any computer might make requests for service, and these might be granted or denied by other computers.

From its beginnings as the ARPAnet, peer networking technology evolved into TCP/IP protocol standards and thence to commercial networks, as both users and developers realized that with standards for interconnecting computers, new ways of doing business would be possible. Low-cost computing could be done close to users and data sources without sacrificing the control inherent in a central data center. Even more radically, with applications like electronic mail, peer relationships could be extended all the way to the personal computer level.

Ethernet

Ethernet was developed in the early 1970s to provide low-cost, high-performance interconnection for hundreds of computers in a data center or on a campus. Its development followed roughly the same path as TCP/IP — initial development by consortium, commercial introduction, market success, and standardization. Combining Ethernet with TCP/IP made it possible for widely separated applications to interact, even across platform boundaries. Thousands of Ethernet local area networks were linked into both enterprise and public network fabrics, and the age of client-server computing began. In the 1980s, government, academic, and commercial enterprises created backbone networks, both to integrate their own operations and to cooperate electronically with other enterprises.

With Ethernet and TCP/IP, enterprises could deploy low-cost personal computers and small servers anywhere. Users were no longer dependent on a central system; they could process data even when not connected. As a result, both processing and data became distributed throughout enterprises. The utility aspect of enterprise computing was diminished further by the relative independence of many departmental and individual computers treated almost as private property by their owners.

Just as Moore's law predicts increased processing speeds, Gilder's law predicts increases in network capacity. In 1995, George Gilder postulated that deployed network bandwidth would triple annually for the next 25 years and that individual link bandwidth would double every nine months. Developments to date suggest that this prediction will be accurate. The elements for a return to utility computing are thus in place — a low-cost commodity (computing power) to deliver and a means of delivering it (ubiquitous networking). All that stands in the way of a return to utility computing is a value proposition (the why) and a catalyst (the how).

The Web and the Return to Utility Computing

In 1990, Tim Berners-Lee, of CERN (the particle physics laboratory based in Geneva, Switzerland), presented a momentous paper describing a hypertext-linked system for information sharing within the high-energy physics community. The attraction was immediate, and events followed rapidly. The year 1991 saw the first version of the hypertext transfer protocol (HTTP) for transferring text between computers of different architectures running different operating systems, which set the foundation for today's World Wide Web.

In 1992, CERN opened access to the World Wide Web to the general public. The number of attached computers grew from 1.1 million in 1992 to more than 6.5 million in 1995. Today, hundreds of millions of computers and other devices are connected to the Internet. Televisions, game consoles, personal digital assistants, and other devices use the Internet to share and find information. Text has given way to images, audio, and video. Live television feeds, real-time multiplayer games, and home shopping are all common. Never has so much information been available to so many people so simply. The Web has moved computing from the domain of business applications to universal availability and utility to everyone. Grandparents, two-year-olds, and everyone in between can enrich their lives through the use of the Internet.

Today, mobile telephones and personal digital assistants use General Packet Radio Service (GPRS) to maintain a continuous flow of information with the Internet. Just as the mobile telephone made voice connectivity independent of an individual's location, the Internet is on the way to placing any and all information at hand no matter where one is or what the time.

The Computing Utility Redefined

The Internet has taken the computing utility concept to a new level by *virtualizing*[6] information resources. Today, anyone can use the Internet to find information on practically any topic without knowing anything about either the infrastructure or the source of the information. It is easy for an enterprise to set up a Web site and conduct business online and for users to buy in the comfort of the home.

Observing the rapid success of the Internet, many enterprises have found ways to exploit the concept for internal use. Browser-based user interfaces obviate the need to install software on every client computer and train users for every new application. The cost savings from not having to distribute, maintain, and update every application on every desktop computer are quite remarkable.

Changes in Computer Systems

The Internet has made delivery of information ripe for a utility. Information is there for the taking. But a utility must always be on; power must be there when an appliance is plugged in. Computers cannot always maintain this level of service — they fail.

From the mid-1990s, mission-critical information services have been protected from computer failure by failover management software (FMS) that monitors continuously and directs applications to migrate or *fail over* to another computer when one is detected. Today, FMS can pool dozens of computers into *clusters*. Applications that run on clusters can move or redistribute themselves if a computer fails, without involving users, who are generally unaware of the specific computer with which they are interacting. In this way, applications are *virtualized*.

All the building blocks for utility computing can be found in today's data center: low-cost processing and storage, the delivery network, a universal user interface (the Web) for anywhere anytime delivery, and user motivation (the value of information and capabilities available on the Web to both the enterprise and individuals). Even the attitudes are in place — Internet users are supremely indifferent to details; they just expect the service to be there when they need it.

---

6. The term *virtualization* is used in many contexts in information technology. It is a layer of software between an application and the computers it runs on that insulates the application from hardware characteristics. A virtualized application can be moved from one server to another easily without user awareness.

Pay-As-You-Grow Data Processing

The 1990s saw a change in the way enterprise computers and storage were designed and delivered. Users looked for hedge strategies against unanticipated growth, and vendors began to design large frames that could be purchased sparsely populated with disk drives, processors, memory, and so forth. As capacity needs grew, additional components could be added to these frames with little disruption. In software, capacity-based licensing came into being — the purchase of a license for a specific number of users. In both cases, users would purchase a "big box" for a relatively low price and add capacity as requirements increased. Incremental capacity might be unlocked with a software license key or delivered as add-on hardware components.

This was progress because it allowed enterprises to pay only for the resources that they required. The drawback was that it bound enterprises to a single supplier. To take advantage of new or superior technology from other suppliers, they would have to write off the big box investment.

Software companies have started to move further — to usage-based pricing.[7] Attempts to introduce it in the year 2000 failed, but with the slower economy since that time, the value proposition for users is increasingly attractive, and pressure on software companies to adopt the model continues. Usage-based pricing would allow, for example, an enterprise that required a database for a one- or two-month project to buy a license just for the duration of the project. In most cases, reducing license cost would also reduce periodic maintenance charges, for further cost savings to users.

7. Usage-based pricing is key to utility computing. With usage-based pricing, fees are charged based on actual days of usage. This model poses a challenge for software companies — how they can maintain revenue streams and at the same time save their customers money. Typically, daily prices tend to be higher than annual licenses, but for occasional use, usage-based pricing can be advantageous.

Utility Computing and the Industry

Major hardware and software vendors have realized the attraction of utility computing to users; most have made it a significant technology and marketing theme. Companies promoting utility computing initiatives include:

- IBM (Autonomic Computing)[8]
- Hewlett-Packard (Adaptive Enterprise and Utility Data Center)[9]
- Microsoft (Dynamic Systems)[10]
- Sun Microsystems (N1)[11]

Arguably, IBM started the trend with its ambitious Autonomic Computing initiative, whose goal is to create a self-managing IT infrastructure of self-configuring, self-healing, self-optimizing, and self-protecting servers, networks, and applications. Autonomic computing has caused other software and hardware companies to think differently about architecting future IT solutions, but it will be some time before it becomes a commercially viable reality.

VERITAS is also promoting a utility computing strategy, described in some detail in Chapter 9. VERITAS' strategy is somewhat unique in being a multiplatform software-based strategy that specifically does not attempt to direct enterprises toward common server, storage, or network platforms. The VERITAS strategy is particularly well suited to system integration companies, several of which are developing IT utility architecture service offerings. As a software-based strategy, it does not require wholesale replacement of existing equipment and is therefore practical from an evolutionary standpoint. As a multiplatform strategy, it provides the system integrator with skills that can be transferred from client to client, no matter what computing and storage platforms the clients use.

Vendors' utility computing initiatives all have the same goal: automatic dynamic configuration of hardware and software resources based on proactive rule-based policies to improve utilization and reduce cost.

But the full realization of utility computing is more than lots of low-cost hardware and software from one vendor. Data centers today

8. http://www.research.ibm.com/autonomic/
9. http://www.hp.com/large/infrastructure/utilitydata/overview/
10. http://www.microsoft.com/presspass/press/2003/mar03/03-18dynamicsystemspr.asp
11. http://wwws.sun.com/software/learnabout/n1/

are inherently heterogeneous. Whether due to legacy or deliberate decisions to run applications on the equipment best suited for them, most data centers have a variety of Linux, Windows, and UNIX equipment in place. Utility computing should make at least some of these resources interchangeable — to allow, for example, excess storage capacity purchased for electronic mail to be co-opted as temporary storage for month-end closings. In a computing utility, the computing and storage resources should be genuine commodities that can be delivered effectively wherever they are needed.

Standards

In an ideal computing utility, applications would be able to find and interact with other applications, as well as processing, storage, database, and other resources supplied by different vendors. Resources would be able to interact regardless of where they came from. The history of computing demonstrates that successful interaction is achieved through standardization. Several utility-related interoperability standards are already in the early stages of user adoption:

- Web Services Description Language (WSDL)
- Universal Description Discovery and Integration (UDDI)
- Simple Object Access Protocol (SOAP)
- The Common Information Model (CIM)
- The Storage Management Interface Standard (SMI-S, formerly known as Bluefin)

While they certainly represent progress, these standards actually compete with each other in some respects, and it will be some time before interoperability standards are mature. Users are beginning to adopt utility computing despite the lack of mature standards. But this is actually encouraging — history shows that user adoption of computing technology drives standards rather than the reverse.

Standards for application provisioning lie further in the future. Today, each system vendor offers its own platform-specific application provisioning facilities. Some software products support multiple platforms. While better than homogeneous solutions, these are still not ideal. Without interoperability standards, users are limited to homogeneous environments, or at best, multiple "utilities" — one for each vendor whose platforms are present in their environments.

Even for a single application, standards are necessary so that data can be processed by different platforms (for example, so an Oracle database can be accessed by either Windows or Linux servers). Without application data format standardization, users will not be able to fully benefit from utility computing.

Into the Future

Across the industry and user community, a related computing initiative is gaining momentum — The Grid. Fully realized, The Grid would link *all* available computing resources together and manage tasks across the entirety. In a sense, grid computing represents the ultimate utility: Users would connect to The Grid, use whatever resources they required, and disconnect. In a sense, The Grid would be similar to today's conventional utilities — turn on the tap and get as much water as you need; make a telephone call and talk as long as you like.

This level of utility computing remains in the future, although there are signs of progress. Collaborative working and resource pooling are in operation today in the pharmaceutical, financial, automotive design, and animation industries. But even there, applications that can take full advantage of grid computing are rare.

Recall the Thomas Watson quote that begins this chapter. Maybe Watson wasn't so wrong. If "the computer" of the future is actually a grid of computers making service available to anyone for running applications, then maybe, just maybe, 20 years' time will see a small handful (five?) of global providers, as is the case with electrical power, telecommunications, and a variety of other utility services today.

Chapter Summary

- The basic concepts of utility computing — centrally provided common services, resource sharing, and accountability — are as old as computing itself.
- The utility model fell out of use when low-cost, easy-to-use computers made it possible for users (business and operating units) to control their own data processing.

- Simultaneously, standardization in networking and availability of low-cost processing and storage have set the stage for a re-emergence of utility computing.
- Other changes to the way in which software and, to some extent, hardware are purchased and used are contributing to the utility computing paradigm.
- Ultimately, standards will be needed for full realization of utility computing, from protocols allowing applications to intercommunicate to management of the utility infrastructure. These will take time to mature, both technically and politically, but user adoption of the utility paradigm will hasten that maturation.
- Utility computing as the concept is currently understood may be just a steppingstone toward an even more flexible information processing environment, commonly known today as The Grid.

PART 2

Getting There From Here

Thus far we have defined the four essential characteristics of a utility (a large user base, a small set of well-defined services, a reliable delivery mechanism, and accountability) and explained why the utility model works for delivering certain products and services and not for others. We have concluded that the utility model should work well for delivering basic information technology services to users (business units and operational departments of an enterprise) and previewed some of the obstacles that IT organizations may face in adopting a utility operating model. This part describes how enterprises can decide on, plan for, and implement an IT utility, and it also presents a hypothetical case study of adoption and some of its effects.

CHAPTER 5

The IT Utility Decision

"Those who do not remember the past are condemned to repeat it."

— George Santayana

In this chapter...

- Steps in a transition from conventional data center to computing utility
- Establishing an information technology baseline
- The cost-benefit analysis and decision to proceed with implementation

Today's typical enterprise information technology operation is a complex of centrally located and managed servers, storage, and applications along with servers and applications managed by operating departments and business units with central IT organizations providing common services such as:

- Purchasing
- Installation
- Hardware and application support
- Backups and other core services

Overlaying this organizational complexity, the need for resiliency means that even smaller enterprises often maintain data far from their main data centers, along with contingency plans for managing it. A large part of the challenge in introducing an IT utility model in an enterprise lies in meeting the needs of both users (getting the job done) and the enterprise (minimizing cost and maintaining competitive position) during and after the transition.

Figure 5-1 illustrates one possible progression from conventional data center to IT utility. The emphasis in Figure 5-1 is on gradual steps that improve operational efficiency and increase IT alignment with business objectives at each stage of the way.

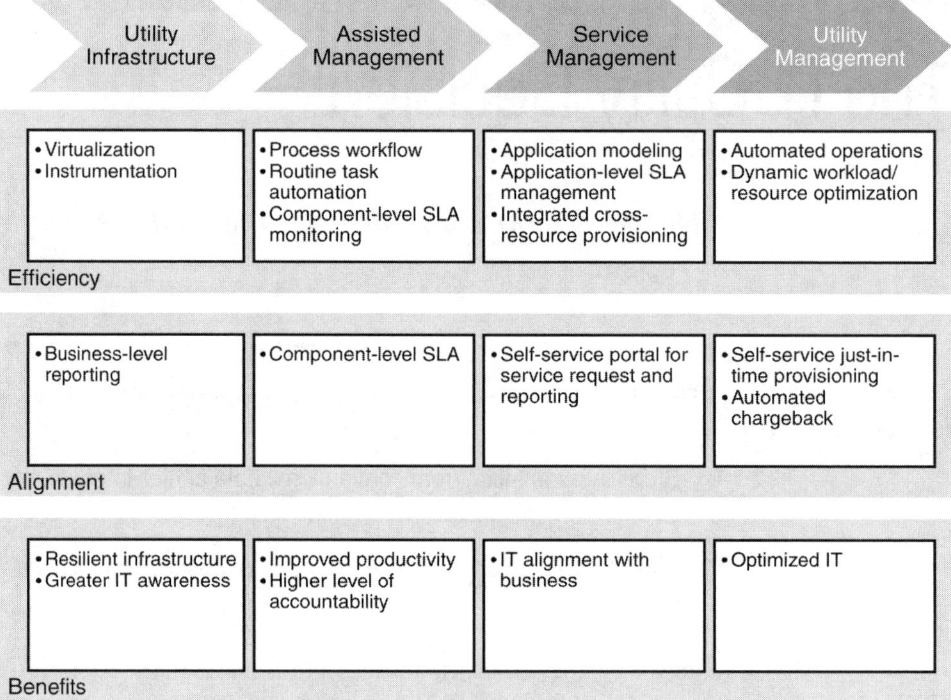

Figure 5-1: Stages in the migration from data center to IT utility

Figure 5-1 suggests a progression of four distinct stages:

- ***Utility infrastructure***. The basic infrastructure for resource sharing (storage virtualization and possibly server virtualization as well) is put into place. From a business alignment standpoint, this is the ideal stage at which to introduce business-oriented reporting of resource utilization to begin the cultural change to IT accountability.
- ***Assisted management***. In this stage, the enterprise starts to act like a utility. Routine tasks like storage and server configuration are either fully automated or follow a strict process workflow. The IT organization starts to negotiate component-level SLAs with users (e.g., guaranteed daily backup rather than two-second application response time). The benefits at this stage are greater operational efficiency and accountability.

- ***Service management***. In this stage, component-level SLAs evolve into more comprehensive application SLAs. Resource provisioning becomes more comprehensive with the introduction of automated tools that discover, configure, pool, and allocate storage and servers. Application modeling tools are introduced, making it possible to estimate the resources required by an application. From a business alignment standpoint, this is the ideal stage for introducing the portal concept of service delivery. The primary benefits at this stage are better alignment of IT with business objectives through service standardization and the beginning of a "pay-as-you-consume" self-service user culture.
- ***Utility management***. In this stage, IT becomes a true utility. Automation enables dynamic deployment of resources for optimal utilization amid changing needs. From a business alignment standpoint, the transition to a self-service user mentality should be complete. Accountability, including the ability to charge users for IT services if appropriate, should be mature.

This four-stage plan strikes a balance between the end goal — delivery of common IT services according to a utility model — and practicality — dealing with the realities of installed capital equipment, existing human skills, organizational culture, and having to conduct business (and process data) as usual during the transition.

The Decision Process

Transforming an enterprise IT organization into a computing utility should not be undertaken lightly. It is a complex process requiring serious introspection, with no guarantee that expected benefits will actually accrue. While the potential benefits are great, particularly for large and complex IT operations, any fundamental change in enterprise operations must be a business decision. In the case of an IT utility, the decision requires a baseline (a comprehensive picture of IT across the enterprise), a cost-benefit analysis, an executive-level commitment, development of a detailed implementation plan, and finally, execution.

The Baseline

In a sense, establishing a baseline is a speculative investment. It makes little sense to undertake a complex and time-consuming transformation without understanding its potential benefits to the enterprise. But it is difficult to estimate potential benefits without knowing what an enterprise's IT deliverables are and ought to be. The baseline collects and organizes this knowledge as a foundation for decision-making.

The Cost-Benefit Analysis

Knowing what IT services it delivers and could deliver more efficiently, an organization can analyze the costs and potential benefits of the IT utility model. A cost-benefit analysis should include both the effect of utility computing on capital and operational expenses and the harder-to-quantify business value of improved quality of service once the IT utility is operating. Improved quality of service may come in the form of less downtime, better application performance, faster implementation and deployment of new applications, or faster reaction to changing business needs. The analysis should consider and evaluate all of these.

The Form of the Utility

There are three basic ways to implement an IT utility:

- ***In-sourcing***. A private utility created and managed by an enterprise's own IT organization to satisfy specific business needs.
- ***Managed private utility***. A private utility managed by a service provider rather than the enterprise's own IT organization.
- ***Public utility***. A common infrastructure and standardized services shared by a number of loosely coupled enterprises, such as operating divisions of a conglomerate.

Which of these is right for a given situation is obviously determined by enterprise goals, internal or accessible design and implementation skills, the financial situation, and the business environment. Whether a utility is managed by internal or contracted resources and whether it is private or shared with other enterprises are separate decisions from the services it should offer and the order in which applications should be incorporated into the model.

The Executive Decision

The cost-benefit analysis is the basis for an executive decision to proceed with a transition to utility computing (or not). The analysis gives executives, who may not be IT experts, a financial basis for decision, as well as a yardstick against which progress and success can be measured. Additionally, specific recommendations for quality of service improvements discovered during the baseline process provide executives with concrete milestones against which to measure progress.

The importance of executive commitment cannot be overestimated. With an IT utility, business units have a menu of standard services rather than choosing unique hardware, software, and operating techniques for each new application service. They often perceive this as curtailing their autonomy. It is generally inadvisable to undertake a transition to utility unless the benefits are appreciated at the executive level, and the importance of the change is communicated throughout the enterprise. Sponsors of utility computing should discuss the transition thoroughly with executives and prepare them to overcome organizational and cultural objections to the move.

The Project Plan

Once a decision is made to move to utility computing, a comprehensive implementation plan is required. The baseline identifies the services that the utility must provide and may identify improvements that could be made under the utility model. The project plan specifies the tactics of the transition, including:

- A schedule for migrating applications to use utility services
- A corresponding schedule for repurposing existing equipment
- Requirements, estimated costs, and delivery schedules for new equipment
- Training schedules for IT personnel and users of the IT utility
- Other logistical requirements, such as incremental facilities, personnel, and support equipment

The transition project plan should be comprehensive, but at the same time, flexible enough to allow for unexpected problems and delays. The plan should include regular progress reviews at which adjustments can be made to accommodate changing conditions or unexpected results.

The sections that follow discuss these steps in more detail.

Establishing a Baseline

Before a transition can begin, it is necessary to capture the state of the enterprise's information technology in a baseline. The IT baseline should include an inventory of capital and human assets, activities, and value to the enterprise. Appendix B contains sample forms that can be adapted for this process. Making an inventory of equipment, software, applications, and human assets and skills is relatively straightforward. Determining the value of IT to the enterprise can be more challenging because the necessary metrics are likely to be inadequate or inconsistent. One of the benefits of utility computing is continuous quantitative assessment of the value of IT to the enterprise.

Making an Inventory of IT Assets

The asset inventory is simply a list of equipment and software owned by the enterprise. For each asset, the inventory should include:

- Physical location
- Age
- Hardware and firmware versions, revisions, upgrades, and patches
- Serial number
- Original vendor
- Support level (under contract, self-supported, unsupported, etc.)
- Owners, users, and maintainers
- Level of utilization (storage occupancy, server and network utilization, backup hardware duty cycle, etc.)
- Original purchaser
- Asset tag number and other internal codes

The inventory should list the IT services in which the asset plays a part and describe how it is used. Finally, original price and residual value should be included to assist in making retirement and redeployment decisions.

Spot checks do not always give an adequate picture of resource utilization. Accounting servers, for example, may be underutilized most of the time but operate at or beyond capacity during closing periods. Servers that process transactions are very likely to have activity peaks that are determined by business policies. Business applications grow and shrink over time, with corresponding changes in resource requirements. Understanding the implicit variability in resource utilization can minimize over- or under-commitment of resources during and after a transition to utility computing.

Finally, an IT asset inventory also determines what is *not* known. By conducting an exhaustive IT inventory, an enterprise may discover that it simply doesn't know what it has or, more likely, the extent to which assets are being used. Monitoring tools are essential to measuring asset utilization; the tools are sometimes present in conventional data centers, but they are often not used systematically.

Overcoming Resistance

It is human nature to resist change, and change in IT is no exception. Some resistance is to be expected as individuals realize what it means to have computing delivered by a utility. Strong executive sponsorship is a must for a successful transition. Often, executive persuasion can help overcome user resistance that manifests itself as passive lack of cooperation with utility architects.

Fortunately, there is recent precedent for dramatic change in IT delivery. During 1998 and 1999, virtually every enterprise carried out an inventory of its IT infrastructure in preparation for (and in fear of) the anticipated "millennium bug." As obsolete and noncompliant assets were identified and replaced, changes in information service delivery were inevitable. While users may have initially resisted them, these changes improved operational efficiency and quality of service, as out-of-date systems were identified and replaced. The transition to a utility model should have similar side benefits; the challenge is in educating users to realize that.[12] Of course, the transition must actually be smooth — it cannot cause serious outages, data loss, or lapses in critical functionality.

12. January 1, 2000, and the dreaded "Y2K scare," is a good case in point. While there was the odd glitch, in general things went incredibly smoothly. Extensive testing and education had the desired effect on IT staff and user morale, and made the transition less traumatic than predicted.

Understanding Enterprise Culture

The baseline gives utility architects a unique opportunity to understand enterprise culture as it relates to IT. Important factors to understand include:

- Who initiates projects that make good candidates for the transition (executive management, the users themselves, or the IT organization)?
- Who typically defines requirements for new information services? How proficient are they?
- When in a project's life cycle is its funding committed? Who has authority to spend budgeted funds?
- What constraints are typically imposed on information service development (e.g., utilization of existing equipment, quantity purchasing, etc.)?
- Who are the "problem" users who habitually submit last-minute requests or frequently change project requirements?
- Is the division of development and operational roles and responsibilities well defined (particularly important for enterprises with many remote employees)?

The move to utility computing is not just about services. It is also about process. Understanding how enterprise culture deals with IT helps architects define services that conform to the culture and are therefore likely to be accepted.

Identifying Utility Services

An IT utility's services must meet the information technology needs of the enterprise that it serves. The first major use of the baseline inventory is to identify common services that are useful to many users. These services might be asset-based, such as mirrored or replicated storage or failover clustering, or they might be process-based, such as server consolidation or data migration. Services might be both asset- and process-based, such as backup, which uses tapes and tape drives but also requires processes to ensure that backups are actually made. Identifying essential services with broad constituencies simplifies the transition by ensuring that the utility is relevant — it delivers value to which users are accustomed from its inception.

A transition to utility computing occurs over time. Not all user needs can be met by standard services at the outset. Thus, as they identify candidates for standard services, architects must also record not-easily-standardized services in order to size the resource pool that they require. Obviously, the size of this pool should decrease over time, as more applications migrate to the utility's standard services.

Utility Scorecards

While the primary purpose of a baseline inventory is to determine which services can be offered and which assets can be utilized by the IT utility, the inventory inevitably captures information about aspects of IT that frustrate users that should be examined for possible improvement. This information is valuable for two reasons:

- It can prevent utility architects from creating services of little or no value to users. If, for example, the inventory reveals that virtually all applications use a weekly-full-plus-daily-incremental backup schedule, and simultaneously that most users are frustrated by recovery times, architects should consider changing the existing backup service to one that offers faster recovery.
- It represents desired improvements that could help prioritize the utility's service developments to maximize positive impact on users.

It is useful to capture this ancillary information semiformally in a kind of utility scorecard. In fact, two such scorecards are useful — one representing user views and one representing the views of the IT organization itself.

The User Scorecard

Important questions for a user scorecard include:

- How do IT services relate to enterprise goals and objectives?
- Do IT services meet availability, performance, and ease of use goals?
- What planning and other preparations are required to use IT services?
- Are there ways in which IT services could be improved?

This information helps architects determine how services might be improved. If the baseline inventory process includes describing how answers to these questions will be used, users should begin to perceive the benefits of receiving IT services in utility form. Moreover, it is human nature to want one's opinions to matter; users will be better disposed toward a utility if they believe they have influence over its progress.

The IT Organization's Scorecard

The basic issue for the IT organization's scorecard is the extent to which IT services are already being delivered according to the utility model. As described in Part 1, a utility usually has well-defined financial metrics and measures its performance against them. In the case of information technology, this helps the IT organization assess the value that it is delivering to the enterprise. New projects are encouraged to use standard services; nonstandard services are discouraged.

To assess the degree to which IT is already following the utility model, it is useful to ask two types of questions. The first type deals with infrastructure:

- How numerous are the resources managed by the IT organization? How many servers, how much storage, and how many network connections are under central management?
- How diverse are the resources managed by the IT organization? How many different types of servers, operating systems, storage devices, network components, middleware, and utility tools are in use?
- How diverse are the configurations supported by the IT organization? Which forms of storage virtualization, clustering, and storage network zones are in use? Are operating systems, applications, and management tools at consistent versions and patch levels? Are resources interchangeable?
- How isolated or integrated are resources used by different users and applications? Are servers, storage capacity, and networks shared among applications? Is data shared by or passed between applications? Can an application's shared resources be isolated if necessary?
- How complex is the IT operation? How many applications do these resources support? (It is worth gathering data on how many people

use or rely on certain applications to determine their importance to the enterprise.)

- How well does the IT organization track resource usage, performance, and cost against SLAs? Does it account for consumption of backup media, tape drives, networks, and other resources? Is software usage recorded? Can at least a notional bill based on resource consumption be assessed against each user?

The second type of question deals with the IT organization's interactions with users:

- Does the IT organization make and honor SLAs with its users? Is performance against SLAs tracked and reported to users?
- For new projects and upgrades, does the IT organization present options to users, or are user requests accepted uncritically?
- Are users formally made aware of the implications of their decisions, particularly with respect to support cost and cross-enterprise performance? For example, are users informed that mirrored storage costs twice as much as ordinary storage or that application availability 24 hours a day, seven days a week requires redundant servers and expensive full-time service contracts?

In a utility environment, users should be made to understand the implications of their choices. For example, a particular operating system might be ideal for an application, but if it is not already supported, the incremental cost to the enterprise can be quite high. Similarly, a user might believe that disk system-based data replication is ideal for disaster protection, whereas the IT utility might be able to deploy software-based replication at little or no incremental cost to achieve similar results.

Using the Inventory

The completed IT inventory must be analyzed to determine what services the prospective utility should offer and in what order. The goal of analysis is to identify the smallest set of services that will serve the largest number of users. Existing services should be examined for possible combination. For example, an analysis of backup services might examine questions like:

- How many different ways does the enterprise have of backing up data, and how many truly unique requirements do they represent?
- Is daily incremental backup with weekly full backup really all that different from daily incremental backup with full backup every four days?
- Must all full backups really be done on Sunday, or could the load be distributed throughout the week to balance load and minimize tape drive requirements?

With an enterprisewide view of which users consume which IT services and in what quantity, utility architects should be able to classify existing IT services as:

- ***Utility services***. These include services delivered to users on an ongoing basis whose usage can be measured. Online storage, backup, processing capacity, firewalls, Web services, and other client access all fall into this category. In an IT utility, these become the services offered and paid for based on consumption.
- ***Routine on-demand services***. These services are delivered when requested by users and include deployment of new storage and computing capacity, changing configuration (e.g., from RAID 5 to mirrored storage), instituting a backup schedule, and so forth. They are analogous to the installation and repair services offered by traditional utilities. Their key characteristic is that they can be delivered by first-level support staff with only basic training and skill.
- ***Consultative services***. These services are also delivered on request but generally require greater skill than routine on-demand services. Examples include implementing applications and databases and designing disaster recovery strategies. These services are delivered by highly skilled and often specialized personnel. An IT utility delivers these services by combining its technology expertise with a user's knowledge of his business objectives and techniques.
- ***Basic infrastructure***. These include enterprise and storage networks, floor space for equipment, HVAC, installation and maintenance, and staff training. Like utility services, these services are delivered to users. They are so basic to operations, however, that it is difficult to apportion their cost precisely to users. They are the IT utility's cost of doing business and must be accounted for as such. As a utility matures, introduction of more sophisticated monitoring tools enable more precise accounting for basic infrastructure services.

Categorizing services in this way completes the baseline process that began with the IT inventory. At this point, utility architects are armed with knowledge of:

- Material and human assets
- Information services and applications required to operate the enterprise
- Common IT services that underpin the delivery of these services
- Users' suggestions for how IT services could be improved or delivered more effectively
- A taxonomy of existing IT services that provides insight into the physical plant, infrastructure, equipment, and human assets both available and required to deliver information technology using the computing utility model

With a solid knowledge base about its operations, an IT organization can make an informed decision to proceed with a transition to utility computing or not by balancing the cost of transition against the anticipated benefits.

Defining New Utility Services

The three key factors in defining an IT utility service are:

- The cost of delivering the service
- The service's availability requirements
- The service's performance requirements

Cost

The cost of IT utility services should be estimated as completely as possible, including capital, real estate, power, cooling, support, personnel, tools, and skill development. Generally, it costs less to deliver a service that is delivered continuously or frequently than one that is delivered once to meet a special requirement (indeed, this is a fundamental argument for the utility model). Particular attention should therefore be paid to economies of scale and the lack of such economies incurred in the delivery of nonstandard services. Service pricing should be set accordingly.

Availability

Information service availability is a complex topic covered in detail in *The Resilient Enterprise*[13] and *Blueprints for High Availability*[14]. In essence, an availability requirement is a balance between a desired level of uptime and the cost of achieving it. If cost were immaterial, all users would demand continuous availability. But availability is not free, so users are forced to choose the level of availability they can afford. As an application becomes more important to its enterprise, the business cost of downtime increases, and increased protection against downtime becomes cost-justified.

More money can buy more uptime, usually in the form of protection against more types of threats. For example, mirrored storage protects against data loss but not against downtime due to server failure. Clustering protects against server failure but not against data corruption. Frequent snapshot-based backup protects against data corruption. All three mechanisms must be used together to protect against downtime due to all three threats.

Service availability should be evaluated from the application user's perspective. Either a person can use an application or he cannot. If he cannot, the application is effectively down, no matter what the cause. Particular care should be taken to avoid single points of failure that can incapacitate services with high-availability SLAs.

Performance

Application performance can be the most challenging part of IT service definition, particularly during the planning stage when little or no experiential data is available. To the extent possible, service performance goals should be defined so that:

- The cost of a service is in proportion to its value to the enterprise.
- Performance can be measured and compared to SLA specifications.

Many IT organizations only measure application performance in response to user complaints. As utility services are defined, architects must be realistic about specifying performance in ways that can be

13. *The Resilient Enterprise*, edited by Paul Massiglia and Evan Marcus (VERITAS Software Corporation, 2002) ISBN 0-9744578-0-9.

14. *Blueprints for High Availability*, 2nd Edition by Evan Marcus and Hal Stern (John Wiley & Sons, 2003), ISBN 0471430269.

measured. In the early stages of a transition like that suggested in Figure 5-1, component service levels are specified. As a utility matures, its performance measurement and analysis capabilities must become more sophisticated to allow it to make the transition from component-level SLAs to application-level SLAs.

Benefit Analysis

Together, the baseline and service definition represent the cost portion of a cost-benefit analysis. Knowing what services it delivers, or ought to be delivering, and knowing their cost (or at least, knowing that it doesn't know) positions an IT organization to estimate the benefits of utility computing. Benefits fall into four categories:

- ***Reduced capital expense***. Initially, the utility should reduce capital expenses through more efficient use of existing assets. New applications may exploit unused capacity in existing hardware and software.[15] As new equipment is required, it can be purchased for the enterprise rather than for individual applications. Enterprise-class servers and storage systems can be utilized if they are most cost effective; "commodity" servers and "JBOD" (just a bunch of disks) storage can be deployed if that makes the most business sense. Finally, by reducing the number of vendors to one or two per component type, an enterprise may be able to negotiate better price, delivery, and service terms for hardware and software.
- ***Reduced operational expense***. Using assets more efficiently reduces operating cost. It costs less to operate fewer servers and storage systems. With more common components, fewer operational skills are required (and service improves because people become more proficient at doing things that they do more often).

  The utility model also encourages automation of mundane tasks, such as allocating additional storage capacity. More automation means fewer administrators and better service due to fewer human errors. Combined with systematic monitoring of performance and availability, policy automation can ensure that service-level agreements are met.

15. To be sure, software doesn't have computing capacity per se. For applications that use server-based licensing, however, multiple instances of the application on a single server can conserve licensing cost.

- ***Reduced downtime***. An IT utility can configure mirrored storage and clustered servers that might not be affordable by independently managed applications. When combined with proper administration practices, these techniques substantially reduce both unplanned and planned downtime.

  Cost savings from reduced application downtime can be quite dramatic. For example, a server that crashes four times a year and takes 95 minutes to restart results in 380 minutes of application downtime per year. Running the application in a cluster can reduce each incident's downtime to five minutes or less, for a total of 20 minutes annually. The value of the cluster is the business cost of six hours of downtime.[16] Running applications in a cluster also reduces planned downtime by enabling rapid migration for maintenance or load balancing.

  By pooling resources, an IT utility makes high availability accessible to more of an enterprise's applications. Data replication and wide-area application failover, for example, are typically only affordable by an enterprise's most critical applications. But a single pair of servers can replicate data for many applications, and a wide-area cluster can likewise make several applications disaster-tolerant.

  Finally, as a utility matures, automating problem detection and response (e.g., failover management software that detects and recovers from server failures without human intervention) further increases application availability by minimizing problem discovery and failover time.

- ***Better performance***. IT utilities improve average performance across the enterprise for several reasons. First, resource pooling makes it possible to match resources to demand dynamically. Is data mining too slow? Add a disk restripe for more bandwidth. Is a Web server handling more users than expected? Use a front-end traffic director to rebalance incoming client requests.

  Second, systematic monitoring can detect degrading performance and raise alerts. A running trace of application response time can

16. Chapter 4 of *Blueprints for High Availability*, 2nd Edition by Evan Marcus and Hal Stern (John Wiley & Sons, 2003) ISBN 0471430269, contains a more detailed discussion of the cost of downtime and the value of high availability.

distinguish momentary peaks from chronic overloads that result in service-level agreements not being met.

Finally, long-term analysis of performance data identifies loading trends, enabling a utility to anticipate and act to prevent resource saturation, avoiding performance problems before users are affected.

The Transition Plan

Assuming that the baseline inventory, new service definition, and benefit analysis result in a decision to implement an IT utility, the next step is planning the transition. Proposed utility services should be prioritized by payback, and the risk in deploying each should be assessed. The combination of payback potential and risk should determine implementation priorities. For example, server virtualization may be a utility's highest priority in terms of potential payback, but unless the IT staff has experience with clustering, the risk of business disruption may suggest that a different service, like backup, makes a better candidate for initial transition to a utility model.

The transition of an IT service to the utility model occurs in three overlapping tracks:

- The service is implemented by the IT organization. Usage monitoring is enabled and standard procedures for users to request the service are instituted.
- The IT organization provides routine or consultative services to reconfigure applications to use the service. For example, if a utility offers a high availability service for applications, it would naturally provide a consultative service to encapsulate applications into cluster service groups.
- As new applications are implemented, users are encouraged (e.g., by pricing) to request the standardized service using standard procedures.

The transition plan specifies the order and timing of these steps for each service, as well as the timing of supporting events like deployment of new hardware and software and training of personnel and users. The plan should also specify the budget for the transition.

Capital Equipment and Logistics

No existing enterprise has the luxury of "starting from scratch" — creating its utility computing infrastructure by purchasing completely new hardware, software, and infrastructure components. Existing equipment and software are phased into the utility and, in some cases, augmented or partially replaced. For example, a hodgepodge of mirrored and RAID arrays might be replaced by a single mirroring service performed by a server-based or network-based volume manager.

These moves must be carefully orchestrated so that applications are not disrupted and quality of service remains the same or improves throughout the transition. Staging includes purchase, delivery, installation, and, most important of all, testing. Every component or service change that occurs during the transition must be rigorously tested without impacting users.

Training and Cultural Change

Architects and executives alike must continuously evangelize utility computing. Additionally, the transition requires more specific training of two types:

- IT personnel must be trained to deliver utility services effectively. Depending on the similarity of utility services to those previously offered, training might be more or less extensive. IT personnel also need training in the utility philosophy — to resist the natural tendency to accommodate user requests whether or not they conform to the utility's standard service offerings. The "let's meet the stated requirement" attitude must be supplanted by "let's figure out how to make it work with standard services."
- Users must be taught to expect a menu of standard services rather than open-ended negotiation when an application is implemented or upgraded. This training is typically informal. More formal training is required when the utility automates its service access portal. The change from meeting with administrators to negotiate IT services to self-service can ease the transition for some users but may be intimidating to others.

Chargeback can be an especially sensitive issue for some users; the utility charges them for resources that they perceive as having formerly been "free." Executive support can be helpful in this respect, emphasizing the enterprise perspective over the narrower departmental one.

Rigid Flexibility

As with any major undertaking, pitfalls will occur during the transition despite the best intentions and most thorough planning. Some events will be beyond the control of the utility architects or, indeed, of the enterprise. Vendors retire preferred products, applications and database software fail to integrate, and business downturns delay planned capital expenditures.

Thus, while it should be as complete as possible, a utility transition plan must also be flexible. It should include regular reviews at which progress can be evaluated and adjustments made to accommodate changing conditions or unexpected results. For the staged transition suggested by Figure 5-1, each stage should include two or three reviews, usually keyed to significant milestones. Reviews should involve both the IT organization and the user community. They also help to assess ongoing user reaction to the utility and change in the IT environment brought about by the transition.

Planning is never really complete for an IT utility. Even after the transition, there will be new applications to deploy and new capacity to add along with an environment of constantly changing technology. Without a comprehensive picture of its users, what they do, and what they want, a utility cannot manage change effectively. An electric company, for example, keeps track of weather patterns, major sporting events, and other demand generators so it can produce or acquire the power to satisfy the demands without wasting resources (and therefore money) or failing to satisfy its users.

Chapter Summary

- The migration to utility computing should be preceded by a baseline to determine what services are required, what equipment, software, and skills are available, and what user requirements are going unmet.
- Armed with a baseline, an enterprise can analyze patterns among users' IT requirements and assess the potential effectiveness of utility computing.

- IT services can be classified as basic infrastructure, utility, on-demand, and consultative.
- A transition to utility computing should be staged. The four stages of the transition are: infrastructure implementation, assisted resource management, service management, and finally the mature utility.

CHAPTER 6

Implementing an IT Utility

"Do not go where the path may lead, go instead where there is no path and leave a trail."

— Ralph Waldo Emerson

In this chapter...

- A four-stage blueprint for implementing an IT utility
- Choosing and managing suppliers and partners
- Internal goals for IT organizations

With the baseline established, executive-level support obtained, and a cost-benefit analysis and project plan complete, implementation of an IT utility can begin. A transition from conventional data center to utility necessarily traverses the four stages suggested by Figure 6-1 (reproduced from Figure 5-1), whether or not they are identified as such in the implementation plan:

1. Creation of the utility infrastructure
2. Assisted management of resources
3. Service management
4. Utility management

Stages in Implementing an IT Utility

The services currently being offered by the data center must be transitioned, one at a time, into utility-style services. For example, backup is a good first candidate for conversion to the utility model because it positions an IT organization to begin assisted management of backup services (stage 3) concurrently with standardizing its online storage offerings (stage 2). As online storage services are phased from assisted management into service management offerings, work on processing service offerings (server virtualization, a complex step for most IT organizations) can begin. Thus, the transition to the utility model is carried out in overlapping steps — one for each service offering.

Each of the four transition stages enumerated in Figure 6-1 (repeated from Chapter 5) benefits users in some way. Most enterprises will find it beneficial to pause between stages to ensure that the implementation is free of unwanted side effects and allow users to absorb the change and appreciate the benefits. The following sections describe the four transitional stages in more detail.

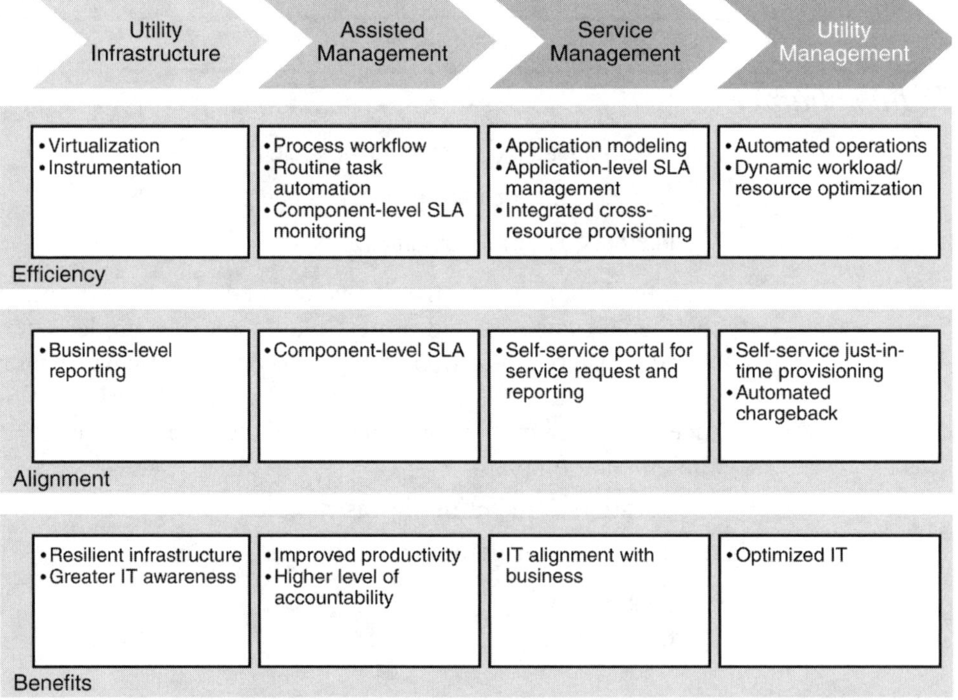

Figure 6-1: Stages in the migration from data center to IT utility

Stage 1: The Utility Infrastructure

An IT utility needs networks with sufficient capacity to support the services it offers and the users it serves. Today, most utility infrastructures include both general-purpose and storage networks, each with sufficient reserve capacity to handle peak demands or unexpected incremental users. The key requirements of a utility's networks are resiliency and flexibility.

Computing and storage resources must be connected to the utility's networks in ways that allow instant redeployment when required. Storage and servers should be designed to meet demands for additional capacity (*not* for physical devices!) quickly and easily (for example, by installing partially populated enclosures).

Enterprise storage systems have been modular for some time. It is quite common for IT organizations to purchase storage cabinets partially populated with disk drives, controller modules, and cache and add components as requirements dictate. A similar, increasingly popular approach to flexible server configuration is to use *blade servers*. These servers are physically compact and mount easily in specially designed prewired enclosures. While the blade server concept meets the hardware flexibility needs of utilities extremely well, using them to full effect in the utility context requires sophisticated software to cluster them and to automate provisioning.

Tools that virtualize storage, servers, and network paths so that capacity rather than physical components can be delivered to users are the third key component of a utility infrastructure. Storage can be virtualized by disk array systems, server-based volume managers, or intelligent storage network components. Servers are virtualized by clustering software, which ranges in capability from static application failover to sophisticated real-time data sharing, dynamic workload balancing, and online capacity expansion by the addition of servers.

Virtualization allows a utility's physical resources to be shared among users, by making it possible to consolidate storage and servers, improving asset utilization.[17] An IT organization that delivers virtual resources to its users can choose between larger numbers of small servers and a few enterprise servers or between enterprise storage systems and *JBODs* to implement the resources. Whatever components are chosen, bulk purchasing for an entire enterprise generally results in more favorable terms.

---

17. Resource consolidation may present opportunities for organizational consolidation. Business units with their own IT specialists may find it more effective to pool specialists in the IT organization to provide utility on-demand and consultative services to the entire enterprise. Often, consolidating IT personnel makes specialization possible, thereby improving the quality of on-demand and consultative services.

As a utility's delivery infrastructure is put into place, it is wise to instrument resources for automatic monitoring of service utilization. While not vital at this stage, service utilization reports will help demonstrate to users and to executive management that IT is taking steps to align itself with the business.

Stage 2: Assisted Management of Resources

Utility services require utility processes for handling user requests. As services are rolled out, users should be introduced to menu-based service requests in place of negotiations for unique services as each new application or upgrade is implemented.

Utility service rollout must be accompanied by education and support. IT personnel must be trained both in the mechanics of delivering services and in user management to overcome the natural resistance to change and help users appreciate the benefits of utility computing. Utility architects must continually evangelize, reinforcing the utility message and emphasizing benefits as milestones are achieved to users and to executive management.

Early in the transition, a "high-touch" approach to users, where architects stay in regular contact with influential users to help make sure they approve of the changes that have been introduced, can help establish a level of comfort with the change. Users can be made more comfortable with changes if there is a pause in progress after each stage of implementation to allow the users to get used to the latest round of changes.

The primary operational change that becomes visible to users during the assisted resource management stage is the institution of component-level service-level agreements (SLAs). Several other less visible tasks can also begin at this phase, including automated service delivery, tape drive reallocation, online storage virtualization, and cluster expansion. The IT organization can begin to deploy policy-based automation and workflow management software. These tools generally take two forms:

- ***Component managers***, such as VERITAS SANPoint Control™, Volume Manager, Cluster Server, and OpForce™ software, that automate storage resource management, storage virtualization, server virtualization, and server provisioning, respectively
- ***Workflow management tools***, such as VERITAS CommandCentral™ Service software (Figure 6-2) and Global Cluster

Manager, that automate service request management and wide-area application failover, respectively

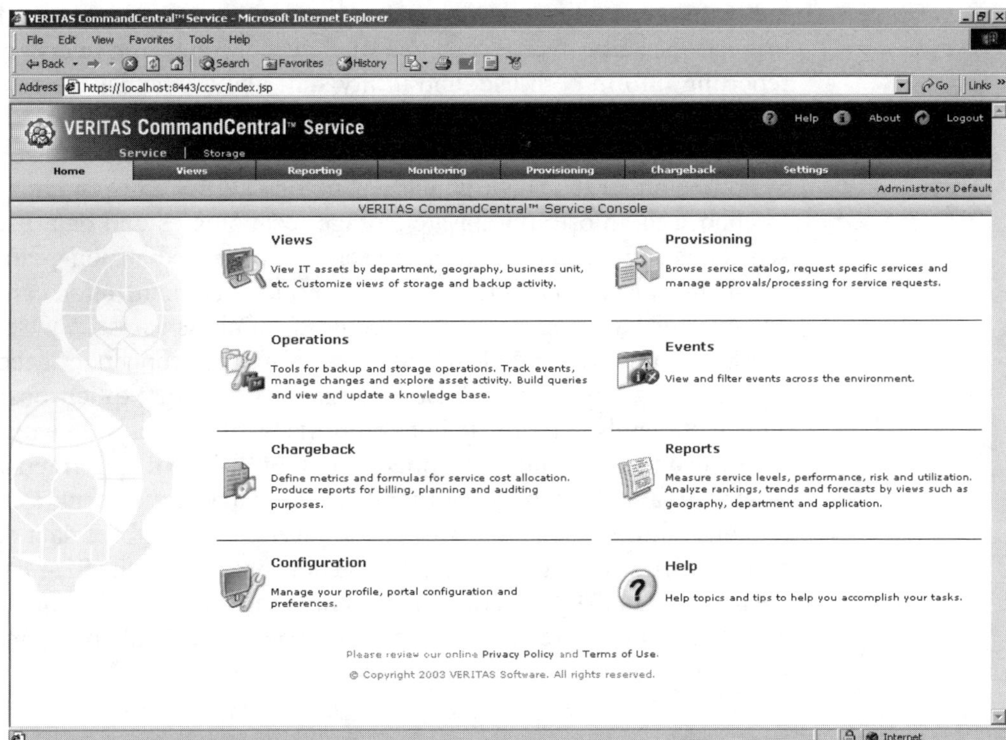

Figure 6-2: VERITAS CommandCentral Service console

Component managers automate component discovery and configuration. For example, a policy might specify that Hitachi disk systems be configured as 50 gigabyte mirrored logical units or that Intel-based servers have Linux operating systems installed. Component managers can execute these policies without human intervention as new disk systems and servers are connected to the utility network.

Workflow administration tools formalize user service requests by tracking request intake, approval, routing, verification of execution, and user feedback. These tools, and the workflow processes they enforce, are the natural evolution of the less formal service request processes instituted during the infrastructure stage.

Monitoring instrumentation installed during the infrastructure stage and utilization reporting instituted during this stage lay the groundwork for service-level agreements (SLAs) covering delivery of services at a prescribed level of performance and availability. For example, a utility might agree to deliver online storage with 99.95 percent uptime over the course of a month, with requests for 10 percent capacity expansion to be met within one hour, up to a maximum of 100 percent expansion from original capacity over the course of a year. Monitoring and periodic reporting inform both user and utility staff about whether the service-level agreement is being met.

SLAs allow an IT organization to act like a utility. Delivering a level of uptime rather than a particular technology allows an IT organization to choose the most appropriate storage technologies and data backup schedules and techniques to meet user needs. The expansion guarantee assists in capacity planning. In both cases, the IT organization can plan and execute based on the aggregated needs of all its users.

Even at the resource level, SLAs reinforce the concept of accountability with both users and the IT organization. An explicit business agreement tends to motivate honest efforts by all parties to live up to it. SLAs also tend to minimize "finger pointing" — the ill-informed accusations of fault that tend to proliferate when a vague agreement results in dubious failure to deliver an ill-defined service. If monitored data shows that an SLA has been met, users should not complain. If the SLA has not been met, the IT organization must compensate the user who contracted for services that were not delivered. Compensation should be defined in the SLA.

Stage 3: Service Management

Once users are comfortable with resource SLAs, evolution to more comprehensive managed service can begin. This stage has the same goal as the assisted management stage — moving users toward SLA-based services — but it does so for entire applications. At this stage, the emerging IT utility should be prepared to deliver *all* of its services (storage, computing, and communication) using a utility model. Services should be virtualized with automated configuration, provisioning, and monitoring.

In the service management stage, SLAs are contracted for applications rather than for components. For example, rather than 99.95 percent availability for the storage devices that hold online retail sales data, a service-based SLA might specify that the online retail sales application will be available 99.9 percent of the time with an average user response time of no more than three seconds over any hour.

SLAs with a user perspective are much more likely to be accepted in the long term. Users generally do not care *why* applications are unavailable or performing badly, only *that* they are inadequate. Resources don't matter to them, only the ability to run their businesses. As a utility matures, users increasingly entrust technology management to it and manage applications from a business perspective. For this stage to succeed, users (and executive management) must trust the IT organization enough to hand over day-to-day operational control of applications.

Managing entire applications to contracted service levels requires sophisticated monitoring tools. Keeping complex application services operating at stringent service level specifications requires not just comprehensive performance monitoring of client access, application, database, and storage but also correlation of performance and availability data, root cause analysis, and, where possible, automatic correction before users even notice problems. Such sophisticated analysis tools have a secondary benefit — they improve an IT organization's ability to plan for future growth:

- They enable the IT organization to optimize asset utilization across the enterprise.
- They provide trend data that can be used to forecast and plan for growth and change.
- They make it possible to model application behavior based on resource models and execute "what-if" scenarios to determine the impact of new applications.

Users can be expected to show greater interest in the utility at this stage, as they increasingly monitor actual performance against SLAs and, in some cases, manage their own resource usage. It is generally in a utility's interest to implement some form of self-service mechanism such as a Web portal so users can submit and monitor service requests and generate activity and usage reports. Such a mechanism increases awareness of the IT utility and gives users a perspective on how others are using IT.

Stage 4: Utility Management

The final stage of the IT utility transition, comprehensive management of the utility, is about optimization: maximum automation of operations and services through policy-based management. At this stage, with user confidence established and benefits being delivered, an IT organization can concentrate on increasing internal efficiency.

Policy setting should begin simply, for example:

- A retail application that generates new data should receive 20 GB of additional storage whenever its available storage drops below 2 GB.
- The last available server in a cluster should never be allocated to the Web service.

Slow, steady progress is advisable at this stage. In a sense, the stage never finishes; it is the mature operation stage, with continual policy refinements improving the utility's service and adjusting to changes in business conditions.

As a utility provides more services and supports more applications, the potential for unintended side effects of policies increases. Policies should be regarded as provisional, with fallback mechanisms remaining in place, until they have actually been invoked — until the retail application has actually had additional storage allocated to it or the Web service has actually failed to acquire the last available server. This strategy will limit the unintended impact of side effects of new policies.

By this stage of operation, users should be accustomed to making the utility's standard services fit most of their application needs, to requesting services through the access portal, and to receiving utilization reports ("bills"). For its part, the IT organization should be using enterprise-level usage reports for capacity planning.

During routine operation, the utility should conduct periodic two-part reviews. For the first part, historical trends should be examined to determine what is working well and what is not. Warning signs include SLAs that are consistently violated, delays in implementing or upgrading applications, and operations or administrative staff stress levels. In the second part, the IT organization should review its findings with key users and identify unmet requirements, user plans likely to change demand, and new services needed.

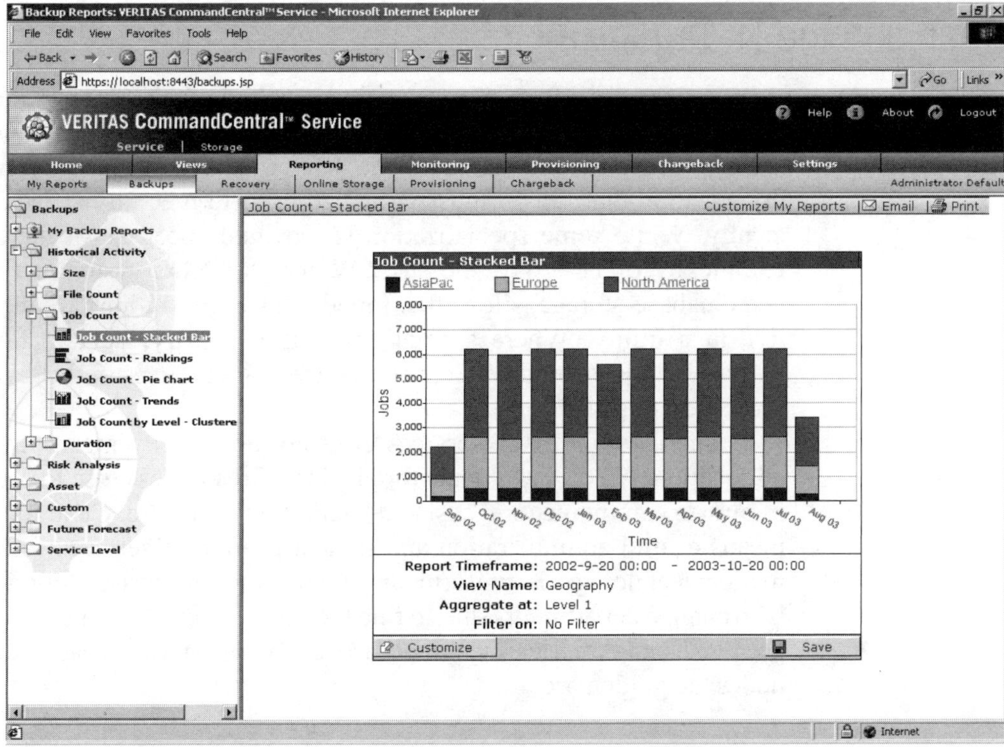

Figure 6-3: VERITAS CommandCentral Service enterprise report sample

An IT utility should periodically analyze and report on its operations to demonstrate to executive management that the following utility computing goals are being met:

- Reduced IT costs through optimal use of capital and human resources.
- SLA-based service delivery, with continuous monitoring and automatic adjustment when service levels are not met.
- Improved timeliness and quality in response to service requests.
- Business-like IT that delivers a small menu of well-understood, predictable services for known cost and reports usage so users can understand the financial impact of service demands and usage.

A successful review should demonstrate that the enterprise IT organization is operating as a true utility.

Changing the IT Organization

A transition to an IT utility must include evolving the IT organization as well as the services it provides. Just as a utility achieves economies of scale by consolidating resources and delivering virtualized services, the organization that runs it must virtualize itself to meet user needs efficiently. While some specialization is inevitable because of the sheer complexity of IT today, the strict Windows-UNIX, system-network, and database-storage, silos often found in IT organizations are ineffective in a utility. Where specialization is necessary, demarcation of responsibilities should be clear so that there are no gaps in the services provided to users.

Centralization of IT services does not necessarily mean physical co-location. All the arguments for placing IT resources close to users to minimize communication cost and latency are still valid. Centralization means central administration and standardization of services so information technology is uniform throughout the enterprise. Individuals who change departments should find the same IT services wherever they go, just as an American visiting Paris or Tokyo knows what to expect under the golden arches.

Changing Users

Making users comfortable as control is taken from them is always challenging, but it is especially so in information technology, where for 15 years users have increasingly controlled their own information services. Today, however, IT is a victim of the success of open systems. Low-cost, easy-to-use computer systems encouraged business and operating units to automate. Only as automation occurred did enterprises realize that computers must be linked as are the business processes they automate. The need to integrate heterogeneous computer systems is causing enterprises to recentralize and making utility computing attractive. The challenge for utility computing architects is to attain the benefits while retaining the user friendliness of departmental systems. Important success factors for the IT organization include:

- ***User focus***. Throughout the utility transition, focus must remain on the user. Utility service implementation order should be based on user needs. In the early stages, personal relationships should be used to build user confidence in the utility. Service portals should be designed for user convenience. Reports should deliver no more and no less than what users want to know. IT technical specialties should match common user requirements such as database or Web expertise. At every stage, feedback should be actively solicited, analyzed, and acted upon to improve alignment with user needs.

- ***Completeness***. A utility works best when it serves an entire community. If a service can be delivered by the utility, it should be. A mature utility should provide all basic infrastructure, utility, on-demand, and consultative services described earlier in this chapter.
- ***Standardization***. Not only should a utility's services be standardized (e.g., one type of mirrored storage, one type of computer fault tolerance, and so forth), but so should its internal processes. Ordering and installation, provisioning of new or incremental services, hardware maintenance and repair, and software upgrade and patching should all be standardized for efficiency, quality, and economy.
- ***Automation***. All routine operations in a utility should be automated, including installation, provisioning, monitoring and fault detection, self-repair, and service request management. Wherever possible, problems should be detected automatically and repaired before users perceive them. With pervasive automation, a utility can control cost and still deliver value to its enterprise.
- ***Flexibility***. While an IT utility should provide stable services, it must also meet unpredictable user demands. By involving users in planning, a utility can minimize the unexpected, but IT is the servant of the enterprise and must meet ad hoc user demands. A utility should maintain a pool of uncommitted resources to meet unanticipated demands. Part of its architecture must be an ability to deploy capacity on demand without adversely impacting service delivery.

  One of the greatest challenges for utilities is keeping technology current while delivering a stable menu of services. An IT utility must be aware of technology developments (it should be someone's job) and periodically review its operations and services in light of what is available on the market.
- ***Accountability***. IT utility services must be accountable. Services should be designed so cost can be unambiguously associated with usage. Inevitably, there will be some common infrastructure (for example, real estate, enterprise network, and IT staff cost), but users should pay only for the services they use, not for an apportioned share of all enterprise IT costs.

- ***Self-promotion***. As a utility creates services, they should be "marketed" to the enterprise. Typically, the incremental cost of providing more of a service is less than that of initiating it, so as more of a service is used, the cost to all users diminishes.
- ***Innovation***. An IT organization must continually seek innovative ways to improve existing services and create new ones. Business changes constantly. If a goal of the IT utility is business alignment, it must anticipate changing needs. User focus groups can identify opportunities for new services. As with any utility, if services don't match their needs, users will eventually solve their own problems, returning to the old inefficient practices.

Partners and Suppliers

Standards-based IT systems have been successful because they do not commit buyers to a single vendor. An IT utility should consider this when selecting suppliers and partners. There should be at least two equally qualified sources for each major type of equipment and environmental software used by the utility.[18]

Partners often assist with consultative services. A potential partner's alignment with utility computing philosophies should be closely analyzed before engagement. Some key questions include:

- Does the partner thoroughly evaluate user situations before offering solutions?
- Does the partner have favorite solutions, or is it open to all available options?
- Is the partner willing to work with the utility's standard services?
- Can the partner move users gracefully from legacy systems to the utility model?
- Can the partner understand and work toward enterprise IT utility goals?

Just as a utility has SLAs with its users, service partners should be bound by SLAs with the utility. These SLAs should clearly specify partner deliverables and ongoing support. Partnerships should include skill

18. Strategies like this can be difficult with demand-based pricing that is constrained by quantity and term guarantees. Until a utility is very sure of a vendor relationship, a utility is usually wise to be cautious with demand-based software pricing.

transfer to the IT organization in the form of thorough documentation and training.

Although they are rare, consulting organizations that are expert in both IT environment and organizational analysis generally make worthwhile partners, especially in the early stages of a utility transition. Such partners can both speed successful adoption and help overcome organizational barriers and user resistance.

Finally, common utility software (like backup) and application products should be "utility friendly." They should be instrumented for usage monitoring and should ideally offer demand-based licensing. Applications should be evaluated for adaptability to multiple enterprise needs before adoption.

Alternatives to Utility Computing

Are there alternatives to utility computing? Certainly one option is to reject the utility model. It is always easier and safer to continue with the familiar than to change. In fact, by implementing the utility model in phases, even adopters continue with the familiar for a time. By offering simple, low-impact services at first and continuing to offer more complex services in a traditional manner, they build user and IT organization confidence.

Not adopting utility computing may be the right choice for enterprises with small or simple IT operations. For large or complex operations, however, analysis will almost always conclude that there are benefits to utility computing.

Outsourcing — contracting with a specialist company to implement utility computing — is an alternative to implementing one's own utility. While this may be the right choice for some, it forces an enterprise to give up control of its IT. Enterprises that are highly dependent on IT should think long and hard about the implications of not developing the in-house expertise required to control this vital part of their business.

A hybrid model — contracting for provision and management of routine services like infrastructure, storage, and so forth, while retaining overall architectural control of the utility — is also possible. Whatever the form, an IT outsourcing decision should be made by executive management, as it is truly strategic for any enterprise.

Chapter Summary

- There are four natural stages in a transition to utility computing: infrastructure implementation, assisted resource management, service management, and maturity. The four stages can be implemented separately for each major class of utility services, with separate timetables. Thus, for example, backup may be at the managed service stage, while the infrastructure for online storage virtualization is just being installed. In all cases, adoption should be on the time scale of the business, rather than that of the IT organization.
- The more mature an IT utility, the more its users are likely to demand reports on utilization so that they can police their own resource utilization.
- As it transforms itself into a utility, an IT organization must continue to focus on customer service, along with standardization, automation, flexibility, accountability, and self-promotion.
- Suppliers for a computing utility should be chosen based on how well they fit the utility model and the enterprise's particular adoption of it. Dual supply lines should be maintained if at all possible, and potential partners should be carefully screened for compatibility with utility goals.
- An enterprise may choose not to adopt utility computing because a cost-benefit analysis fails to show benefits, or it may choose to outsource its IT operations. This decision must be made at the executive level because relinquishing control of information assets may have implications beyond the scope of the IT organization.

CHAPTER 7
Implications of Utility Computing

"Hoc erat in votis"[19]

— *Horace*

In this chapter...

- Indirect impacts of utility computing
- Beyond the application environment: enterprise benefits of utility computing
- Changing technology and the future of utility computing

Utility computing is not just about computers, networks, or applications; it's about all of these things, but more importantly, it's about processes for using them effectively. Utility computing is also about money — ensuring that money spent on IT delivers business benefits. In summary, utility computing is an IT architecture for the future. This chapter examines changes likely to be brought about by utility computing — on individual users, on corporate behavior, and on the IT organization itself.

Change and the Individual User

The benefits, costs, technology, and processes of utility computing, as well as the implementation cycle, have been discussed. But what of individual users, the knowledge workers who rely on information technology to do their jobs? What changes will utility computing make in the way they do their work?

Ideally, individual users won't notice the change to utility computing at all. At most, they will observe subtle improvements in service.

19. This is what I wanted (or literally, this was among my prayers).

Information accessibility will improve as availability increases. Unplanned coffee breaks while Web servers restart will become a thing of the past. Days without information because new servers are being installed or applications migrated will disappear. Performance will improve as components and infrastructure are used more effectively. No more drumming fingers on the desk waiting for an e-mail response. No more lapses in attention because the CRM system is so slow.

In global enterprises, "follow-the-sun" applications that stay close to active users by migrating around the world during the course of a day become possible, reducing both latency (visible to individual users) and communication cost (visible to management). By ingraining the concept of flexible, dynamic redeployment of resources in the IT organization, utility computing makes it natural to consider radical modes of operation like this, which would be unthinkable under a conventional IT model.

Change and the IT Organization

Of course the most pervasive changes brought about by utility computing will be within the IT organization itself. The utility elevates attention on IT to the executive level. But executives won't just pay attention to IT; they will think about it differently. Rather than listening to a CIO justify more servers, storage, or other obscure technical components, executives will be considering operating departments' spending for IT services that are defined in business terms. Their decisions will be based on whether the cost of services is commensurate with their business value.

Budgeting

Utility computing also changes IT budgeting significantly. At the outset, an IT utility's own budget may pay basic infrastructure costs that are difficult to ascribe to users. These costs include components (such as management consoles), physical infrastructure (component frames, backbone network wiring), and overhead staff (core IT management, administration, consulting, help desk). The remainder of the budget (the majority) is negotiated with operating departments and business units against delivery of specific services such as online storage, backups, and so forth. A utility's long-term goal, however, should be to apportion as much basic infrastructure cost as possible to users.

Perhaps one of the greatest challenges to a transition to utility computing is legacy systems. It's unrealistic to think in terms of instant wholesale replacement of IT systems and procedures. Legacy systems must be maintained, upgraded, and migrated gradually to the utility model. In some cases, adoption occurs only when systems are replaced. One useful strategy is the one adopted by Flossco, the hypothetical company in the Chapter 8 case study — making the high cost of maintaining legacy systems apparent to users through cost-based pricing. For example, if a legacy system is the only user of a certain platform, that system's users should pay the entire cost of supporting the platform — maintenance contracts, specialist personnel, training, upgrades, etc. If users observe that services functionally equivalent to what they are receiving cost less on the utility menu, they should be motivated to move their legacy applications to the utility model.

Building User Relationships

An IT utility's users are operating departments and business units. While users should appreciate the improved service levels enabled by utility computing, there may be tension around accountability and chargeback. In particular, high-volume users may react negatively to the exposure of their cost of doing business to the rest of the enterprise. To overcome negative reactions and persuade users of its value, a utility must deliver increased value in several forms:

- ***Reliability***. Perhaps the greatest benefit an IT utility can deliver is reliable operation. The highest compliment a user can pay information technology is not noticing it. IT has achieved utility status when it's "just there" — when users think of computing, storage, and communication services in the same way as the wall outlet or the water tap. Of course, delivering reliable computing services is more challenging because of the rapid pace of information technology change. A utility must formulate operating procedures that deliver reliable services as the technology that provides those services continuously evolves.
- ***Economy***. When departmental IT costs are visible at the executive level, there is strong motivation to minimize them — to "look good" to the organization. An IT utility must provide excellent, detailed reporting, both periodic and on-demand. In addition to reporting

individual departments' return on investment, a utility can increase user confidence by explicitly reporting on enterprise savings due to resource sharing and economies of scale.

- ***Agility***. By standardizing services and making resources interchangeable, an IT utility should be able to respond to ad hoc user requirements faster and better than a conventional IT organization. Again, a utility must not only do the job right, but must also, through prompt and detailed reporting, make it clear to the rest of the enterprise that it is doing the job right.
- ***Simplicity***. In most enterprises today, information technology is a prime source of complexity and user frustration. As it achieves economies of scale by standardizing services and sharing resources, a utility must also make the inherent complexity of enterprise computing transparent to users. Not only are sophisticated tools a must, but care must be taken that the utility's outward face — the view it presents to users — is simple, logical, and consistent. As Chapter 5 suggests, this may require an extensive "hand-holding" period during the transition, with IT representatives guiding users as they become familiar with the utility model. But eventually, an IT utility must transition to a self-service portal, designed with extensive user consultation.

Managing Complexity: Automation and Abstraction

The only way for IT organizations to deliver "more with less" is to automate. Today, IT organizations routinely automate tasks like installing standard software images on notebooks, server backup, and application startup and shutdown, but they lack the trust in technology to automate more sophisticated functions, even when tools are available. Tools for data center automation have existed for some time but have not gained full administrator confidence. Hardware and software component vendors must deliver automation tools that not only work reliably but also build administrator confidence (for example, by recognizing anomalous system behavior and advising on corrective action). At a later stage, when trust has been built, corrective action can be automated.

There are bright spots on the horizon — automation in data centers is increasing. Automatic sparing in storage systems and failover clusters are two examples of significant policy-based actions that administrators are willing to automate. Today, there are even more sophisticated tools that can, for example, automatically provision storage and servers based on observations of performance trends. IT organizations are starting to deploy these tools, taking basic provisioning one step further by "pushing" needed resources to applications without human intervention.

Abstraction is another mechanism for managing complexity. Storage has been abstracted for a decade or more under the heading of virtualization. Clustering abstracts applications from the servers they run on so that servers can be interchanged with no effect on applications (and more importantly, with no effect on users). Components of a virtual storage device or server can be swapped out with no effect on applications or users. Virtual device capacity can grow (or shrink) as required; data and processes can be replicated without applications or users being any the wiser.

Changing Technology

Part of the impetus for utility computing today is feasibility — the industry is delivering new technologies that make enterprise computing more modular than ever before. This section examines trends in servers, operating systems, storage and storage management, applications, and software licensing that impact the delivery of utility computing today and will have even greater impact in the future.

Servers

Blade servers are finding their way into the enterprise. The blade server concept is simple — easily configurable prewired racks of interconnected small servers (blades) made from commodity components. A blade server may be equipped with more storage or more processors according to requirements. Rudimentary management software to coordinate the servers' operation completes the picture. The blade server concept is attractive for partitionable applications for several reasons:

- ***Disposibility***. Blade servers are inexpensive and easy to install. If one fails, it can be discarded and replaced. Stocking a few extra servers can eliminate expensive maintenance contracts.
- ***Modularity***. It is not necessary to fully populate a blade server rack from the outset; servers can be added as capacity is required.
- ***Economy***. Beyond the low cost of the servers themselves (stemming from the commodity processor and support chips on which

they are based), savings occur in several other areas, including space, power, cooling, and maintenance.

- ***Computing power***. The low power consumption of blades should not be equated with low computing power. Some blades contain two or four multi-gigahertz processors and gigabytes of memory; they are as powerful as the enterprise servers of only a few years ago.

Industry estimates predict that over a million blades per year will be sold by 2006.[20] One significant inhibitor to growth is the lack of standards, and these are highly likely to fall into place in the near future. Other potential obstacles that may prevent widespread adoption of blade computing include the extraordinary heat output of a rack jammed with blade computers and the weight of a fully loaded rack. There are unconfirmed reports of fully loaded racks causing data center floors to collapse under their weight.

Operating Systems

Today, most blade servers are based on Intel-compatible processors. The choice of operating systems is essentially Windows (for servers), Linux, and Solaris. For several years Windows has predominated, with Solaris having a lesser presence. More recently, Linux is being considered seriously for enterprise applications.

In addition to blade servers, Linux runs on a wide variety of processors, from PDAs to mainframes. Its cost is low (although unsupported "free" Linux is generally uninteresting to enterprises). Companies like Red Hat, SuSe, and others that specialize in distribution, support, training, and consulting are gaining credibility. The maturation of Linux has motivated database and application vendors to port their software, and today Linux is a contender for serious data center use.

Commercially viable Linux creates an interesting opportunity for computing utilities. Since both Linux and Windows run on Intel-compatible servers, the choice of server is no longer inextricably bound to the choice of operating system. An Intel-compatible blade server can be provisioned dynamically to run either operating system according to need. This both simplifies a utility's internal operations (fewer suppliers are needed) and increases its range of service offerings (its platforms can run either Linux or Windows-based applications and middleware).

20. "Blade Server Forecast" by Jeffrey J. Hewitt (Gartner Inc., 2002).

Of course, adopting this strategy has its own complexities. Version and patch control has historically been a Linux weakness, especially when compared to Windows. Without rigorous change control over all facets of the IT operation, there is no guarantee that a server will in fact run a given application. Adoption of blade (or other low-cost) servers as the basis of a utility's processing service must be accompanied by ongoing configuration control, preferably with automated configuration management and provisioning.

A recently introduced generation of automatic provisioning software makes it possible to *clone* running servers. Provisioning software like VERITAS OpForce™ keeps detailed records of operating systems, middleware, and revisions and uses them to automatically provision "bare" servers with application-specific configurations. With automatic provisioning, servers can literally run Linux one minute and Windows the next, with applications installed and started automatically — *all without human intervention*. Being able to adapt server capabilities to requirements automatically dramatically increases a utility's ability to fully utilize its assets, improve quality of service, and lower cost.

Storage

Of course, moving applications from server to server to meet changing requirements is only practical if their data can move with them. Storage devices that are directly connected to one or two servers effectively make utility computing impossible. Storage area networks (SANs) that interconnect all of a data center's servers and storage devices make it possible to exploit blade or commodity servers for utility computing.

Today, storage networks are based predominantly on Fibre Channel, a technology developed specifically for that purpose. Fibre Channel is designed for high data transfer rates with low protocol overhead on relatively static network topologies. While unarguably the enabling technology for storage networks, Fibre Channel has an inherent disadvantage — it forces the IT organization to maintain two network technologies, one for storage and one for all other enterprise communications.

At the outset, storage networking required its own technology because the enterprise network technology of the time had neither adequate bandwidth nor sufficiently low protocol processing overhead for enterprise data traffic. Today, this is changing. Gigabit Ethernet (GbE) is becoming the standard for enterprise networks with 10 GbE rapidly emerging. Enterprises and developers are using GbE and 10 GbE for storage as well as enterprise networking. A new storage protocol, iSCSI (SCSI protocol running over Ethernet), looks especially promising for use with blade servers. Reducing the number of network technologies required will reduce both component cost and staff and skill maintenance cost for computing utilities.

Storage Management

Managing online storage has become a full-time role in many IT organizations. Automated policy-based storage provisioning is a must for future IT utilities. Storage provisioning requires discovery (finding storage devices as they are added to the network), configuration (creating mirrored or other virtual disks), and allocation to applications or server groups (adding virtual disks to applications' storage network zones). Adding a policy engine to these basic facilities enables storage network management software to "do the right thing" with storage devices as they are added to the network or with ad hoc application requests for additional storage capacity.

Finally, the storage network itself is becoming intelligent. Today, storage network switches can replicate data to remote locations and perform backup data transfers without interrupting application service. IT organizations have an expanded menu of technology choices for implementing storage services.

Of course, more options mean more complexity. The number of storage devices and interconnections in a data center of even moderate size make automation a necessity. Fortunately, vendors are integrating individual management applications to make it practical to administer complex enterprise storage environments.

Applications

When existing applications run in a well-managed computing utility, they just run better. Being able to move applications to cope with faults or changes in demand improves performance and resource utilization across the data center. Ultimately, however, utility computing needs utility applications to take full advantage of the environment.

Applications will change subtly with utility computing by the addition of monitoring and management instrumentation, either from within or without. The change won't affect users, but it will have a powerful effect on the utility itself. The need for monitoring tools is fundamental to accountable service delivery. To charge for consumption, it is necessary to measure it. To meet a service-level agreement, it is necessary to know about and correlate user, processing, storage, and network activity and faults. Today, usage is monitored outside the application for the most part — by operating system or storage monitors and logging facilities. In the future, applications will tend toward self-monitoring, integrating with standards-based data center provisioning and management software.

Today there are few broadly applicable parallel applications like Oracle's Real Application Cluster, although there are some specialized ones particular to individual companies or industries such as oil exploration. Next-generation applications will be tailored to blade servers — capable of running simultaneously in multiple coordinated instances spread across dozens of servers. This change will not occur overnight. Middleware tools that enable application instances to cooperate are required, as is the education of the software engineering community in the techniques required by distributed applications and environments.

Finally, applications must integrate better with operating systems. During installation, they must sense whether the operating system has required components and upgrades installed and hardware features are adequate for successful operation and take action if they are not — all without human intervention. Since most enterprise applications are designed to run on multiple platforms, standards for exchanging and acting on this information are clearly required. While few of these capabilities are available today, application vendors are becoming aware of the issue and developing ways of accommodating the utility generation in the future.

Software Licensing

Application licensing today is not particularly well-suited to utility computing. Many application licenses are node-locked (specific to a server), making it difficult to utilize alternate servers for load balancing or failover. In a large IT utility, an application might run on any of dozens of servers at different times. Licenses bound to specific servers are impractical; applications must be able to run wherever they are provisioned. Requesting a new license key from the vendor each time an application moves to a different server is simply not an option.

Operating system licensing is similar to application licensing. With automatic provisioning, a utility's server might run different operating systems at different times. Operating systems may run on servers of widely differing capacities. Vendors must modernize licensing, adding monitoring and management to their operating systems. Usage-based licensing would be the ideal. As usual, tools are key, but in this case, operating system vendors themselves must provide them. Such tools must not only meet vendor needs (collection of revenues due for usage), but also the needs of IT utilities. Reporting must be sufficient to give utilities and users a running picture of costs incurred.

Of course reinstalling an operating system every time an application migrates is impractical, especially if applications share server capacity. Ultimately, utility computing will require intelligent provisioning tools that can match available server resources to application requirements, whether this means provisioning a server whose hardware meets application requirements or adding an application to an already-running server or cluster.

Security in the IT Utility

Data access security is vital to any enterprise. Security needs order, but order is rare in constantly changing environments. In traditional data centers, proper security is often viewed as detrimental to user service. IT organizations face a difficult choice between delaying service to users and compromising security.

Most IT security specialists would agree that security must encompass access requests, authorization, change control, audit trails, automated task execution, monitoring, exception alerts, and escalation. Utility computing requires all of these and therefore seems to be an ideal starting point for implementing comprehensive IT security. Security can be built in as easily as any other requirement when a service is defined. Once a service is implemented, its operational procedures naturally reflect designed-in security. The following paragraphs discuss how utility computing might affect various facets of IT security.

Service-Level Agreements

A service-level agreement should define *all* the parameters of a service, including security. An SLA should specify both expected security levels and user obligations (for example, password change frequency and refraining from unauthorized downloads). Most services should be able to follow a single security specification; enhanced security might be offered as part of a premium service where warranted.

Service Requests

In an IT utility, users' service requests result in electronic tickets that follow a workflow defined as part of the service definition. Approvals are a natural part of request workflow, and are permanently recorded with each ticket. Approvals may be required for any reason — financial responsibility, confidentiality, legality, and security. The service request ticket is the natural place to record management authorization for access to applications or services. Because tickets include a complete history of requests, they are an ideal basis for security audits and other reviews.

The enterprise IT security team must become an active participant in the workflow system. Security-related requests must be approved, escalated, or rejected promptly. If the security team is not properly organized, staffed, and trained, users and IT staff will continue to view security as something to be circumvented in the interest of "getting the job done." Conversely, if the security team responds promptly and is easy to work with, the overall image of security is likely to improve. And if things go really well, users might even start asking for extra security on their own!

System Administration

Some of the most frustrating IT security problems are the direct result of poorly administered systems that, for example, grant permissions too liberally or allow weak passwords or nonstandard accounts and directory names. Utility computing may not eliminate these, but it can help in two ways. First, all new applications will "start clean," since they will be deployed using utility standards and procedures. Second, the workflow system will force changes to be in accordance with utility procedures, which should always include security checks.

Monitoring and Escalation

Managing events has always been difficult for security teams. Firewalls, virus and intrusion detectors, and other security-related tools are typically network or system administrator rather than security responsibilities. In an IT utility, security teams should be informed of events automatically as a part of an escalation rota, and security-related actions can be defined for administrators who initially field alerts. Additionally, event logs and workflow system request tickets make it possible to audit sequences of events, a capability that is critical in diagnosing problems and identifying security "holes."

Vendor Tools

In a conventional IT operation, each new application is a special case as far as resource configuration is concerned. By standardizing services, utility computing improves quality of service because each new configuration repeats techniques (including security) that are known to be valid. For example, to deploy a new application, blade servers running already-vetted operating systems and middleware can be added to an existing rack. While the application itself may have unique security requirements, the security team need not validate the security of operating system, network, and storage configurations that it has never seen before.

From Cost Center to Value Center

Centralized IT budgeting and inadequate accountability have led inevitably to poor utilization. In the boom economy of the late 1990s, this was usually tolerable; money was plentiful, and there was a tendency to overestimate IT project requirements, purchasing for peaks in demand expected several years in the future.

The economic downturn that began in 2000 highlighted enterprise "big spenders;" invariably IT departments were on the lists. Controlling and reducing IT spending became an issue in almost every enterprise. Initial savings often came from staff reductions. Only later was it realized that underutilized assets meant that significant growth capacity was available if it could be harnessed.

Storage and server consolidation reduced administrative cost, but excess capacity and peak application demands remained. Matching the two without sophisticated tools to monitor load is difficult. A new generation of comprehensive monitoring tools like VERITAS i^3 software technology (VERITAS Inform, VERITAS Insight, and VERITAS Indepth) helps system administrators find and exploit these mismatches. VERITAS i^3 software monitors server and application performance. In multitier applications, VERITAS i^3 software correlates events in different tiers and automates root cause analysis.

These same tools make precision usage accounting at the department and project level possible. Combined with usage-based software licensing to eliminate "shelf-ware" (software that is paid for but sits on a shelf uninstalled and unused), they reduce the administrative cost of information technology substantially. Fully mature utility computing will enable IT organizations to go even further and reallocate resources dynamically to accommodate peaks in demand without large expenditures, further reducing cost and improving return on investment (ROI).

Chapter Summary

- Utility computing is likely to change the way an enterprise operates beyond the data center.
- Individual users of IT should either not notice the change to utility computing or, if they do, notice it in positive ways like improvements in service.
- The most immediate effects of utility computing are on the IT organization itself. Budgeting changes — instead of a monolithic budget with crude cost allocation, the IT organization budgets for basic infrastructure and "sells" its services to business units and operating departments. The long-term goal is to allocate the entire IT budget fairly to users. Automation becomes essential to managing internal complexity and making it transparent to users.
- Changes throughout computing technology are instrumental in enabling utility computing. Blade and other inexpensive but powerful servers make server virtualization possible. Storage virtualization is expanding from individual storage devices to the entire data center. Operating systems are becoming interchangeable as the Intel processor model becomes predominant, and automatic provisioning tools are gradually making automation of the utility a

reality. The next steps are development of standards for the utility environment and implementation of these standards in applications.

- Security becomes a paramount concern as IT utilities virtualize computing and storage services. Fortunately, several precepts of the utility model actually provide the opportunity for improving both security procedures and the acceptance of strict security processes by users.

CHAPTER 8

Flossco Adopts Utility Computing

"There are many paths to the top of the mountain, but only one view."

— Harry Millner

In this chapter...

- A (hypothetical) large company's rationale for adopting utility computing
- The utility implementation process
- Results of the company's shift to utility computing

The preceding chapters describe IT utilities' operating techniques and their adaptation of those techniques to enterprise information technology. But after all the work to change the way IT operates, what are the long-term implications for the IT organization and, more important, for the enterprise it supports? Managing the change can be challenging, but the rewards are well worth the effort.

Whether an enterprise is a manufacturer, a service provider, a government, or an educational institution, utility computing significantly increases its control over resources and accountability for their usage. Improvements in service stemming from adoption of the utility model will make the departments and employees who conduct the enterprise's business happier and more supportive of the IT organization.

In many enterprises, information technology is a frequent concern at the executive level, primarily because of its cost. Often, IT has the largest departmental capital budget. In some companies, it accounts for as much as 10 to 15 percent of the employee population, making it a major expense as well. This chapter examines how utility computing can affect the overall operation of an enterprise through the example of Flossco, a hypothetical company that makes and sells dental floss.

The Flossco Company

Flossco (2002 revenue US$1.7 billion) is a medium-sized manufacturer of consumer products specializing in oral care, the second-largest manufacturer of dental floss in the world. They have offices in several locations and countries, but most manufacturing is done in facilities in Montana (in the northwestern United States). Flossco employs 18,000 people worldwide, with 16,000 in the United States. They compete with the giants of consumer products, including Unilever NV, Proctor & Gamble, and Colgate-Palmolive, in a slow-growth market that includes floss, toothpaste, toothbrushes, soap, and shampoo.

Flossco's organization has four product divisions with profit and loss responsibility, as well as marketing, engineering, manufacturing, sales, and the usual corporate functions (executive management, finance, human resources, legal, facilities, and information technology).

Information Technology at Flossco

Flossco's IT operations are concentrated at the company's headquarters campus. The chief information officer manages an IT department of 1,900 employees, 1,500 of whom work at headquarters. The IT department has three functional groups: application support, business support, and infrastructure administration. The application support group includes database administrators, application specialists, and system analysts. The business support group includes a help desk and a team of business analysts for each of the product divisions. The infrastructure administration group includes system and network administrators, security officers, operations staff, a backup team, production and change control managers, and a storage team responsible for disk arrays and SANs. The infrastructure group supports Windows, Linux, and proprietary UNIX-based systems. There is a work request ticketing system used by the help desk and change control teams, but not by the rest of the IT department.

IT Budgeting Practices

As is conventional IT practice, Flossco's IT department was responsible for the entire IT capital equipment budget. The IT department based its annual budget requests on experience and estimates of growth for the coming year. Much of the capital budget was spent in anticipation of expansion — unassigned storage, network capacity, servers, and backup equipment that was expected to be required in the coming year.

Occasionally, special projects would result in special budget appropriations, as for example, when the company opened a new plant to manufacture a new line of polymer film floss. For the most part, however, budgets for business initiatives belonged to product divisions and were not accompanied by incremental IT budget.

When the company's annual results were tabulated, the IT department did not receive much information about which business units and departments were using its services, so costs were allocated using educated guesswork. Capital equipment cost was rising at an average of 25 percent per year and IT headcount by about 10 percent. Occasionally, in difficult economic times, the company would reduce capital and headcount spending by 5 percent or so, but these cuts did little to check long-term growth of IT cost, especially for capital equipment. Expense and capital spending increases had been exceeding the company's revenue growth for an extended period.

The Decision to Implement

Flossco's executive management realized that this level of IT spending growth was not viable for the long term. What was worse, the few usage metrics that existed were insufficient to determine the reasons for growth in sufficient detail to do anything about it. In an attempt to regain control, the CIO proposed a utility computing vision, which the company's executive committee decided to implement in three key areas.

The CIO proposed conversion of network, processing, and storage services to a utility model. The CFO and CEO agreed, on the condition that equipment and software would not be replaced wholesale, but instead would be migrated to a utility service model. The CIO made it clear that new capital purchases would still be required (probably of a different nature) but did commit to flat capital spending for the period of the changeover. In exchange, the executive committee agreed to allocate significant startup funding for utility management software.

The CIO proposed that the imprecise cost allocation system be replaced with direct billing of users for IT services, and that each product division and overhead department should budget for IT services and "pay its own way." Rather than the IT department carrying the entire budgetary load, each business unit and department would budget and be assessed for the cost of IT services used, and therefore overall company spending would not increase. The goal was to make each department's actual IT cost clear at the executive level.

The CIO estimated that the cost of change would be recouped within 24 months, based on an assumption that "business as usual" would result in ongoing 25 percent annual increases in capital expenditure and 10 percent increases in staff. By agreeing to flat capital and expense spending for two years, he was in effect saying that diverting those funds to a shift to the IT utility model would result in no incremental IT expenditure for two years, with savings beginning to accrue at the end of that period.

After extended deliberation, the executive committee agreed on a project budget, which was less than the cost reduction expected from the attenuation of growth. With this smaller budget, the IT team faced a considerable challenge. Conversely, if they succeeded, the return on investment for the transition to utility computing would not be as difficult to achieve.

The Implementation

The CIO selected members of the infrastructure group to define and develop the services, along with an advisory council of application and business support employees. As might be expected from the makeup of the team, services were defined in terms of technology, not applications. The team was asked to deliver detailed service definitions, deployment and provisioning procedures, operations and escalation procedures, cost estimates for implementation and ongoing operation, and service-level agreements for each service it defined.

Network Utility Service

The team was able to define a client network service that ran on a single platform (the IT department had previously standardized on a network vendor) and provided desktop and remote connectivity. Networking within the data center was considered part of the processing service; its definition and cost would be built into that. The team considered defining a disaster protection service using network-based long-distance replication but elected instead to include disaster protection in its premium storage and server offerings.

Storage Utility Services

After evaluating user requirements, the team determined that three storage services would be needed:

- A Gold service using arrays configured for highest performance and availability at the expense of cost
- A Silver service stressing availability over performance
- A Bronze file access service with minimal built-in fault protection and no emphasis on performance

Technologies appropriate for all three services were already present in Flossco's data centers. The team suggested using enterprise-class disk systems configured as mirrored arrays for the Gold service, lower-cost arrays equipped with smaller, slower disks and less cache for the Silver one, and network attached storage (NAS) systems for the Bronze file access service. The Gold and Silver services could both be implemented using Flossco's existing storage area networks (SANs); the Bronze file access service would use newly configured subnets in the company's existing network infrastructure and could be augmented by additional network components if required.

The team strongly recommended that no direct-attached storage service be provided. Storage connected directly to individual servers would be supported only on an exception basis, and users would be encouraged by cost incentives to migrate to Gold or Silver service. The team carefully analyzed storage and SAN performance and reliability characteristics and came up with uptime and performance guarantees for each of the three services. Table 8-1 summarizes the parameters of the Flossco storage services.

Storage Services	Gold	Silver	Bronze
Failure Protection	mirroring	RAID5	none
Response Time	< 10 ms	< 30 ms	< 100 ms
Throughput	up to 50 MB/s	up to 20 MB/s	up to 5 MB/s
Backup Schedule	weekly full 6-hour incremental	weekly full nightly incremental	weekly full nightly incremental
Backup Retention	7 years	1 year	3 months
Cost	$0.15/GB/mo.	$0.08/GB/mo.	$0.02/GB/mo.

Table 8-1: Flossco utility storage service parameters

While backup could be considered a separate service from online storage, the Flossco team determined that there was a strong correlation between online storage service requirements and backup requirements, so each storage service was defined to include a corresponding backup service. Weekly full backups with snapshot-based incremental backups every six hours were specified for the premium service. For the normal and file access services, weekly full backups and nightly incremental ones were specified, with data inaccessible during the backups. In addition, the premium service included remote replication of data to a recovery center to be established in one of Flossco's out-of-state locations.

Processing Utility Services

As might be expected, processing services were more complex to define due to both the range of user requirements and the available technology choices. The team finally decided on three tiers of processing service for each of the three operating systems used within Flossco (Windows, Linux, and UNIX):

- **A Gold service for Flossco's most critical applications**. Gold service was defined as availability clusters within a single data center protected against disasters by long-distance clustering technology. Gold processing service would normally be selected along with gold storage service.
- **A Silver service for important but noncritical applications**. Silver service was defined as two or more servers clustered for failover within a single data center.
- **A Bronze service for noncritical applications**. Bronze service was defined as servers not protected by local or remote clustering. If a server providing a Bronze service failed, recovery would consist of provisioning and deploying a replacement server and restoring data from a backup if necessary (for example, if the entry-level storage service had been selected for the application's data and a storage failure had accompanied the server failure).

The significant factor in these service definitions was that applications would no longer be guaranteed their own servers but rather a processing service at specified levels of performance and availability. The servers delivering the processing service might (and generally would, it was believed) be shared with other applications that had contracted for the same service level.

The team determined that with Flossco's existing and planned applications, Windows, Linux, and one proprietary UNIX was the minimum number of platforms that had to be supported. The decision was based both on current use and on the market availability of "blade" servers supporting those operating systems. The expectation was that as existing servers aged or workload expanded beyond their capacity, more modular replacement or additional servers would be installed, gradually improving the smoothness of scaling.

A second vendor-supplied UNIX system was excluded from the utility processing service set, even though it was in use in Flossco at the time. Again, the team recommended cost incentives to encourage replacement of existing nonstrategic systems with the utility offerings on which they had standardized.

Tools

Because automation and accountability were two benefits that Flossco expected to gain from utility computing, it was important to instrument the planned services and automate maintenance. The team decided that for their purposes, server-based tools were the most appropriate rather than tools hosted on storage or network devices, which tended to be limited to managing the components hosting them. Four categories of software tools were recommended:

- ***Monitoring***. This included both basic processor and I/O utilization monitoring, which is part of most operating systems, tools for detecting long-term trends such as rising average processor or I/O utilization, and analytical tools for correlating trends and events in different parts of a distributed system and performing root cause analysis. Sophisticated monitoring tools are a prerequisite for automating redeployment of resources and usage accounting, so money spent in this area would have high payback.
- ***Automation***. Automation tools come from a variety of sources, so this category was the most challenging to identify. For example, storage virtualization tools (RAID systems, volume managers, and smart switches) are usually capable of discovering new disks, configuring them, and provisioning them according to predefined policies. Servers, on the other hand, are typically provisioned by one set of tools (like VERITAS OpForce™ software) and deployed by

another (clustering software). Flossco's architects determined that automatic storage provisioning was feasible for them, but separate tools with human intervention would be required for server configuration and provisioning, at least in the short term.

- ***Accounting***. With adequate performance and utilization data collection, accounting becomes the routine analysis and summarization of raw data. While not a challenging technology problem, accounting does require meticulous attention to detail. In general, it is usually more cost effective to purchase professionally developed and maintained tools than to create (and implicitly commit to maintain forever) special ones if at all possible. Flossco's architects specified monitoring tools with extensive analysis and reporting capabilities.
- ***Workflow***. Finally, a utility must keep complete and detailed records of its operations. In particular, the progress of service requests must be accurately tracked to guarantee that user requests are met reliably and on time. Again, this is not a challenging technology problem, but it does require attention to detail and coordination with other tools, such as accounting, so, for example, users can be charged for on-demand and consultative services performed on their behalf. Flossco chose a workflow system that could accommodate utility, on-demand, and consultative service requests, as well as help desk requirements.

Schedule

The Flossco team recommended a phased transition to utility computing, beginning with network services followed by storage and, finally, servers. At each stage, they recommended a three-month period of stable utility operation before embarking upon the next stage. The intention was twofold:

1. To identify shortcomings in newly introduced utility services so that the Flossco IT organization did not find itself trying to fix problems in one set of services while simultaneously implementing another set
2. To gradually accustom users to dealing with utility services, thereby increasing the likelihood of acceptance over the long term

In addition, the team suggested a six-month period of stability following the transition in which no changes to the environment would be made.

This period was to be used by the IT organization itself to ensure that interactions between the different utility service components were smooth, operational procedures were as efficient as they could be, and so forth. The team also recommended that during the same period, utility operations be evaluated for possible further improvements in efficiency through additional tools or alternative operating procedures. The idea was that after the six months, users would have become accustomed to the utility model, so internal improvements could be implemented transparently to them.

Results

Flossco's transition to utility computing was generally successful. There were a few unforeseen events, but overall the transition was smooth and planning for additional and upgraded IT services would go ahead. The following sections describe both expected and unexpected outcomes of Flossco's transition to utility computing.

Nonstandard Services

Even as the storage service was being migrated to the utility model, some applications that had not yet been migrated required new or additional storage. In a few cases, storage was installed with the realization that it would have to be reconfigured later as one of the standard services. This was generally viewed as a minor annoyance rather than a serious detriment to progress.

While the Gold, Silver, and Bronze services were defined to meet a broad spectrum of needs, there were a number of users whose needs they did not meet. These tended to be for applications for which Gold-type functionality was appropriate but for which the software stack did not support the Gold services defined. The team proposed to use pricing to motivate users to migrate to the standard services.

Cost Allocation

The Flossco team realized from the outset that fair allocation of costs would be challenging. In practice, assessing the true costs of services delivered to users was even more difficult than expected. For example, a disk array might be used by more than one user department, with some of its installed storage capacity available for use and some potential capacity as yet uninstalled in the frame. Each user should clearly be billed for capacity consumed, but what about the cost of the installed but unused capacity and the fractional cost of that part of the frame in which capacity had not yet been installed?

The team determined that a simple prorating of total cost was both the easiest and most equitable way to bill for shared storage. This scheme did, however, mean that the IT budget continued to bear a significant cost for partially unallocated equipment. The team anticipated that over time utilization would improve, decreasing the IT department's share of hardware cost.

The team also anticipated that charging user departments for IT services consumed would result in more accurate initial forecasts. The initial utilization of new equipment would be high, and the share of cost borne by the IT organization would be correspondingly low. Additional capacity would be added to partially populated frames as required by users.

User Acceptance

One of Flossco's unexpected challenges was getting users to actually use the utility services. The architecture team assumed that once Flossco as a whole had accepted the concept of services rather than private resources, user departments would quickly contract for the utility's standard services as they became available. This was not the case. Even with SLAs, which had not been available before, users were reluctant to embrace the new model. Users expressed concern that committed resources would not be delivered, performance would be inadequate, or promised growth would not be delivered. A leap of faith was required but was not immediately forthcoming.

The three-month period between service implementations was of great help in building user trust. Hesitant early adopters found that they were indeed treated as customers, and their service requests were met faster than they had been previously. Gradually, the user community came to trust the concept of shared hardware, and the adoption rate increased. As more users adopted the utility services, executive management saw utilization improve due to resource sharing and began to approve requests for incremental purchases more freely. This accelerated the acceptance cycle.

Implementation Time

Shorter implementation time for new applications was an expected benefit of utility computing that actually did materialize for Flossco. By asking users to select virtual resources from a fixed list, rather than specifying unique solutions for every application, it became possible to use existing capacity (hardware, software licenses, and network ports and bandwidth) in many cases instead of purchasing and installing new components. Even when it was necessary to purchase incremental capacity, reordering known components was much faster than the previous mode of selecting, purchasing, installing, and configuring unknown ones. Moreover, as the IT organization's skills with the standard services grew, configuration, provisioning, and troubleshooting became faster as well.

Marginal Cost of IT Services

Marginal cost is the cost associated with delivering a single additional unit of a service like online storage or computing. Standardization of services and service levels reduces marginal cost for three reasons. First, purchasing components in higher volume tends to reduce the unit cost of components used to provide the service. Second, staff familiarity with and automation of standard services both tend to reduce administrative cost. Third, improved utilization means that a given complement of hardware and software can meet the needs of more users, reducing unit cost still further.

Clearly, low marginal costs are economically efficient. When published in the form of utility "prices," they discourage waste because they make users aware of the impact of decisions. While in fact Flossco's transition to utility computing reduced the marginal cost of providing all of their utility services, the benefit was difficult to convey to users at first because users had no basis for comparison — prior to the utility implementation, there had been no effective chargeback. Users did not know whether marginal cost was lower or higher than before. Executive management, however, had a global view of corporate finances and could clearly discern savings.

Utilization

The baseline that justified Flossco's shift to utility computing highlighted low average utilization of computing resources across the enterprise. Pooling physical components and allocating virtual resources to users increased Flossco's IT average component utilization from 40 percent to over 60 percent, with the promise of going even higher as more new applications were implemented over time. Flossco's cost of resources was reduced by a third, with room for additional improvement. As a result, the team was asked to plan a further resource consolidation involving the company's remote data centers.

A result of higher utilization is an improved rate of amortization — more effective use of resources spreads their cost across more applications, resulting in greater business value to the enterprise.

Profitability

Utility computing did not make Flossco's IT operation into a profit center per se, but IT did become a value center. Understanding expenses and knowing which user departments were using which IT services and in what quantity made a significant difference in Flossco's bottom line.

The IT utility delivered value for Flossco because it made business units more profitable and helped operating departments control their costs. Making their true IT costs visible allowed business units to make business-aligned decisions about "how much computing was enough" instead of reflexively demanding more IT. The amount of time required to implement new services decreased because both decision and implementation times became shorter. These factors combined to make Flossco's business units more responsive to competition and therefore more profitable.

Overhead Costs

The transition to service-based IT incurs nonrecurring costs. Some are obvious — IT staff training and effort expended to develop new processes and install new tools can be quantified. More difficult to quantify is the cost of persuading users that utility computing is beneficial to them. In Flossco, this included all four business lines, operating departments from purchasing to accounting, and, even though utility computing was the CIO's brainchild, the IT department itself. These one-time costs were accepted as the cost of the transition, with the expectation that downstream savings would result in payback many times over.

After the planned transition of network, storage, and computing services, overhead costs remained within the IT department. Not only were some functions not standardized as utility services, but some operations (such as wiring new network connections) were difficult to account for in true utility style and remained part of the IT budget. The architecture team's expectation was that in time, more of the central IT budget would become allocable to users of IT services, and so the ongoing overhead costs were accepted for the time being.

Despite the overhead costs, the IT organization as well as the enterprise as a whole gained a much greater insight into the cost of information technology and, more importantly, how IT cost aligned with business benefits delivered.

Customers and Clients

Two distinct groups of clients benefited from Flossco's utility-based IT services. The first is obvious: Uuser departments within Flossco realized improved service levels and faster implementation of new applications. The second, less obvious group is the customers of these user departments. This group consists primarily of people and organizations external to Flossco. They experience better performance and improved uptime in their interactions with the company. Without realizing it, they also benefit from faster rollout of new information services, as explained in earlier sections.

As another secondary benefit, the IT department was able to roll out new internal service offerings using existing hardware reprovisioned for the new services. The first of these was expansion of backup service to include notebook backup. Flossco had previously rejected notebook backup, primarily because of the difficulty of apportioning cost. Utilizing reclaimed online storage capacity and investing in specialist software allowed the IT organization to offer nearly transparent notebook backup to paying clients across the company.

Partners

Partners can be important assets in converting a traditional IT department into a utility. Flossco engaged a consulting company to assist with the definition of a storage architecture on which services could be based. The company selected had conducted similar engagements before and had useful experience in implementing utility infrastructure.

But the unsung heroes among the partners in Flossco's IT utility implementation were individuals from different organizations within the company who participated in the architecture team. By building a cross-functional team including all parts of the company that would be affected, the IT organization lowered barriers to acceptance and, more importantly, provided all users with trusted contacts with whom they could raise and discuss concerns.

Chapter Summary

- Flossco is a typical large, but not gigantic, company whose information technology costs were spiraling out of control with little accountability. A visionary CIO believed that utility computing could solve the cost problem without degrading service.
- The CIO proposed creation of utility services for network access, online storage (including backup), and processing. The proposal was made to executive management and was accompanied by a budget request and hard guarantees of payback expressed in terms of IT budget caps.
- The utility architecture team consisted of a core of individuals from the IT organization augmented by an advisory council of users from throughout the organization. This strategy not only tended to align utility services with actual user needs but also improved acceptance because user departments had trusted contacts throughout the development and implementation phases.
- The implementation was phased; one service was implemented at a time, with three-month periods of stability between them to make sure that the newly implemented services were stable and to allow users to become accustomed to them.

- The transition was a success, resulting in Flossco planning to move more of its information technology to the utility model. There were unexpected consequences, both positive and negative. One slightly negative consequence was the size of the base IT budget after the transition, due both to the difficulty of allocating IT infrastructure cost to users and to the number of nonstandardizable services that the IT organization was obliged to support. On the positive side, secondary users of Flossco's information services were pleasantly surprised by improvements in performance, reliability, and function, as resources freed up by the utility were employed to implement additional information services.

CHAPTER 9

VERITAS and Utility Computing

"By recognizing the need to separate connectivity from applications, we have the opportunity to unleash the power of the marketplace that has served so very well in computing and in the Internet."

— Bob Frankston

In this chapter...

- The evolution of VERITAS from storage management to application management
- The VERITAS integration strategy for automating IT utility operations
- Achieving user satisfaction with service-level agreements

VERITAS Software Corporation is expanding its utility computing product set. The company completed four major technology acquisitions in 2002 and 2003, each extending the company's utility computing technology portfolio. These acquisitions are the opening moves in a long-term strategy aimed at making VERITAS the industry's premier enabler of utility computing. This chapter describes the current and emerging VERITAS strategy for platform-independent utility computing.

Pressures on IT Executives

A typical information technology executive faces pressures from three quarters:

- Business functions that demand more applications, more data, and shorter implementation times

- Executive management, which demands cost containment or reduction
- Increasingly complex technology environments that require more highly skilled system, storage, and database administrators in increasing numbers

IT departments are often regarded as one of the least efficient areas of an enterprise. 60 percent idle time for a fleet of cars would be regarded as gross inefficiency. Yet a surprising number of enterprises' online data storage is 40 percent or less utilized. No enterprise would tolerate 70 percent unused office space, but a recent survey of a large telecommunication company's servers found average utilization at less than 30 percent.

With data like these, it is no wonder that executive management thinks that IT efficiency is poor. As a result, IT budget and capital expenditure freezes are common. CIOs are constrained to capital investments that can be recouped almost immediately. Increasingly, CIO compensation is linked to IT cost reductions, and expectations of service remain fixed.

Results of the Pressure

Thus, IT organizations are expected to deliver more services at less cost, while infrastructure complexity and administrative requirements are both on the rise. Moreover, user expectations of availability are rising as well. With its promise of improving storage efficiency, SAN technology is one potential (partial) solution. But SANs increase infrastructure complexity (and therefore management cost) even further. SANs are a new infrastructure layer that require technology, tools, and skill sets. Similarly, Linux and low-cost servers reduce capital expenditures but require more administrative staff with new skills; the cost of these can quickly outweigh hardware and operating system savings.

The pressure to do more with less in an increasingly complex and highly available environment is focused squarely on IT executives. They must provide information systems that do more, cost less to build and maintain, and are part of an integrated IT fabric that is more robust than ever before. The job of an IT executive is indeed challenging and, it seems, growing more so every day.

The VERITAS Strategy

VERITAS' strategy is to help IT organizations cope with these pressures by delivering technology that increases resource utilization and operating efficiency, decreases time to deployment, and improves the level of service delivered to business users. In essence, VERITAS' strategy is to deliver software components that enable enterprises to implement the IT utility model in their data centers. The following sections describe how VERITAS' traditional technologies, augmented by the company's strategic technology acquisitions, enhance its utility computing capabilities.

Storage Virtualization

Historically, VERITAS has been known for storage management technology. The company has approached the market by partnering with system vendors like Sun Microsystems and IBM, which deliver VERITAS foundation technology along with their platforms. More recently, the company has become the leader in storage virtualization, both simplifying and enhancing management of online storage.

VERITAS delivers storage management technologies like multipathing, which both balances data traffic and improves robustness. As networked storage has become more popular, VERITAS has expanded automation with SANPoint Control™ software, which dynamically detects new storage devices on the network and uses predefined policies to configure and allocate them to SAN zones, servers, and applications.

VERITAS is currently extending storage virtualization technology into the network itself, with VERITAS foundation components that run in intelligent storage switches from Brocade Communications and Cisco Systems. These switches make it possible to configure and provision storage from within the SAN itself and deliver virtual storage to application and database servers that are completely unaware of its physical makeup. In the future, more sophisticated forms of virtualization, including replication and checkpoints, will also be available at the fabric level. Moving storage virtualization into the SAN simplifies the application server and lays the groundwork for server virtualization.

Application Availability Management

Historically, VERITAS has focused on keeping enterprise data available with its data protection (NetBackup™ and Backup Exec™ software) and foundation (Volume Manager and File System) technologies. As these became successful, the company expanded into application availability with VERITAS Cluster Server (VCS), which automates application management. Today, VCS users deploy clusters of as many as 32 servers to gain efficiencies of scale and decrease application outages.

VERITAS application management and data protection technologies are integrated with each other and with major applications. For example, NetBackup and Backup Exec agents integrate Oracle and other database backups with an overall enterprise backup strategy. As another example, VERITAS Database Edition/Advanced Cluster (DBE/AC) provides a foundation for Oracle 9i RAC parallel databases.

VERITAS has established market leadership in all of these areas — data protection, storage virtualization, storage resource management, and clustering. In some markets, VERITAS market share exceeds that of hardware and operating system vendors.

But neither IT nor applications are static. As more applications are delivered on the Web, 24x7 availability is becoming a basic requirement. Web-based user communities often have no way to communicate directly with application service managers. Their services must simply be available all the time.

Application Performance Management

In addition to availability, IT utilities must also manage the performance of applications that use their services. Individual users need access to information "at the speed of thought." To use computers optimally in the conduct of business, users need responses to arrive before they lose their concentration.

VERITAS entered the application performance management arena by acquiring Precise Software Corporation in 2003 after exhaustive market research revealed that Precise had market-leading application performance management (APM) technology. At the same time, VERITAS acquired automatic server provisioning technology through the acquisition of Jareva Software and its flagship product, OpForce.

To appreciate the uniqueness of VERITAS' APM technology, it is helpful to imagine the path between users and data. An application user typically uses a Web interface that runs through a J2EE server, an application server, and a database server, which accesses data on storage devices. VERITAS APM technology, delivered as a suite of products called VERITAS Inform, VERITAS Insight, and VERITAS Indepth (collectively VERITAS i^3™), deploys agents at each point on this path to monitor, correlate, analyze, and, in some cases, improve application performance in real time.

VERITAS' i^3 technology makes it possible to visualize performance graphically at each layer of a distributed system "from URL to SQL" and correlate data from different layers to determine root causes of performance problems. If performance degrades (usually detected by i^3 before users notice degradation), i^3 helps administrators identify root causes and take corrective action rapidly and accurately.

Through its graphical interface, VERITAS i^3 software allows administrators to quickly isolate root causes of performance problems to network, application, or database. The Indepth component drills into applications to:

- ***Determine*** why performance is degraded, down to the database query level
- ***Suggest*** potential solutions, such as adding an index to a table
- ***Predict*** the result of applying the remedy

VERITAS' i^3 technology eliminates "blame storming," the natural tendency of database, network, and system administrators to assert that performance (and other) problems do not stem from their respective links in the electronic chain.

With VERITAS i^3 software, VERITAS has expanded fault protection-based availability technology to include performance-based availability technology. This expanded focus supports the IT utility model, because from a user's perspective, there is little difference between a poorly performing system and one that is down.

The combination of VCS and VERITAS i^3 software technologies enables dynamic infrastructure changes such as moving application instances from an overloaded system to a less heavily loaded one, balancing load. Administrators need no longer wait for something to fail or users to complain before taking action; they can automatically recognize performance problems and take action before users are even aware of them.

Storage Resource Management

Moving to enhance its utility computing facilities, VERITAS acquired two storage resource management-related product sets:

- ***Storage Reporter***. Comprehensive storage utilization reports
- ***StorageCentral™***. Proactive storage resource management

These products, when integrated with each other and with other VERITAS technologies, will represent the most comprehensive utility computing software on that market, automating storage, server, and application management.

It's relatively easy to determine which storage devices are allocated to which servers or applications. To manage storage resources effectively, however, it is also necessary to know *how* storage is being used. VERITAS Storage Reporter reports on storage utilization, and StorageCentral™ software enforces policies that restrict the types of objects that can be stored on a per-user basis. Users can be blocked from using particular file systems or prohibited from storing or accessing, say, MP3 files.

Enterprises migrating from Windows 2000 to Windows Server 2003 may find that the migration is the perfect time to install StorageCentral software and set policies that limit the data being migrated, shortening the migration and "cleaning up" the target data.

Automated Server Provisioning

The next level of sophistication in utility management of applications is automation. Because it directly addresses administrative cost, automation usually represents the greatest opportunity to reduce IT spending. Analysts estimate that in a typical IT department, staff cost can approach 60 percent of the entire budget, making it an obvious target for reduction. One of the most effective ways to control staff cost is to automate routine tasks, freeing staff to spend its time on more strategic and challenging ones, such as implementing additional applications.

In early 2003, VERITAS acquired Jareva Software, whose OpForce technology automates server installation and provisioning. Automated server provisioning is a necessary step toward server virtualization, employing a similar model to the company's automatic storage virtualization technology.

In keeping with VERITAS' product strategy, OpForce™ software is heterogeneous — it supports Intel servers for both Microsoft and

Linux operating systems, as well as Solaris and AIX, with HP-UX planned for the near future. OpForce software works by discovering servers as they are connected to the network and installing "thin kernels" on them. The OpForce kernel inventories processors, memory, local storage, network cards, and host-bus adapters. By knowing the properties of available servers, OpForce software can preconfigure suitable servers with *golden builds* — proven images production applications. Servers can be preconfigured or configured dynamically according to changing conditions in the data center.

Automating the installation, configuration, and provisioning of servers is particularly important with Linux; enterprises are deploying thousands of low-cost Linux servers to replace enterprise servers running proprietary operating systems.

OpForce technology can also automate service pack installation in environments with dozens or hundreds of Windows servers. A service pack can be installed on one server and that server's configuration replicated throughout the environment. Using VERITAS Cluster Server technology, applications can be failed over to alternate servers as OpForce software performs upgrades. OpForce software reconfigures a server with a different operating system and middleware. This is important in the Intel space, where Windows and Linux can both be automatically configured with OpForce and corresponding applications. OpForce software automates server configuration and provisioning so that servers can be deployed as needed.

Tying It All Together

Each of the VERITAS technologies described in these sections leads in its space. Together, these technologies represent opportunities for users to increase IT efficiency and move toward utility computing. But it is VERITAS' strategic intent to integrate these technologies more closely with each other and with other VERITAS technologies. The possibilities are perhaps best illustrated with an example, shown in Figure 9-1.

In Figure 9-1, the VERITAS Insight component of VERITAS i^3 software detects that user response time is rising unacceptably (1). The VERITAS Indepth component determines that the application's Linux file server is saturated and requests that the OpForce software provide a file server-capable system with greater capacity. The OpForce software locates a server with suitable hardware (2) that currently has Windows installed, takes a snapshot of the Windows configuration (in case it must be restored in the future), and shuts down the server. Next, OpForce installs software to transform the server into a Linux file server (3), using a Linux file server golden build as a guideline for installation.

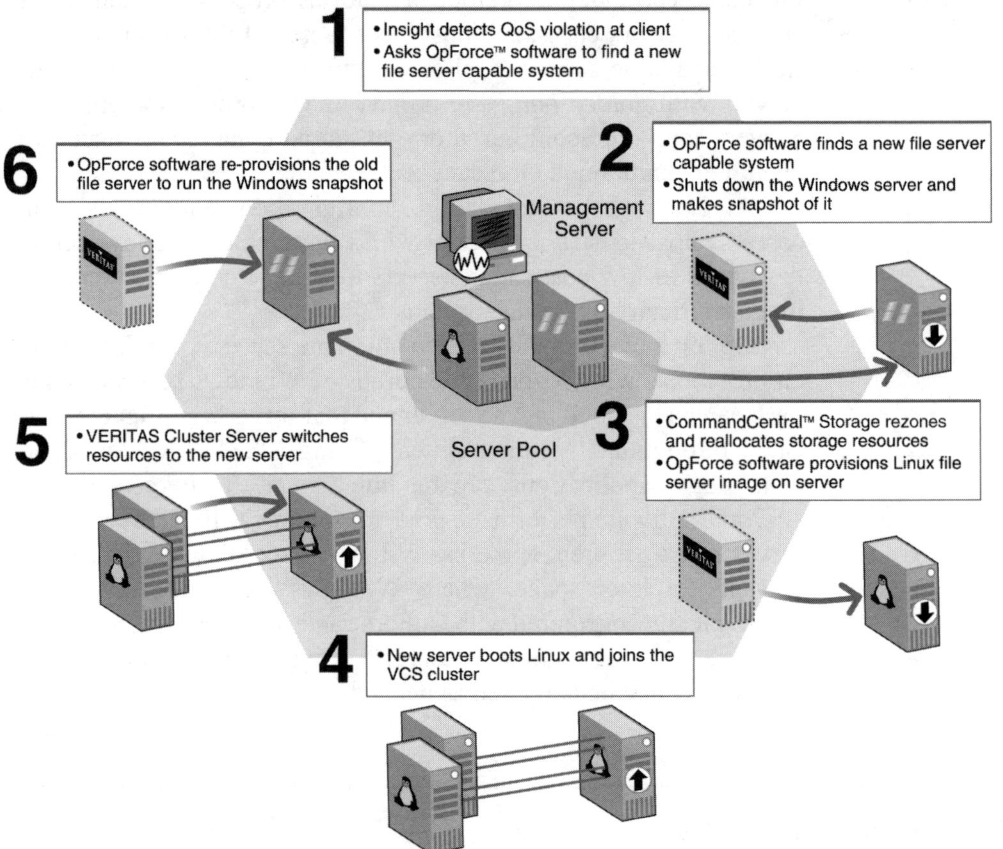

Figure 9-1: The VERITAS automatic provisioning strategy

At this point the newly configured Linux file server is booted, and control is given to VCS (4), which adds it to a cluster that includes the saturated file server to be replaced. VCS fails the file server application over to the newly added (more powerful) server (5). When failover is complete (6), the more powerful file server satisfies client file access requests. As the figure also indicates, the OpForce software might configure the less powerful server with Windows in case it is needed for other purposes.

Everything indicated in Figure 9-1 can be done without human intervention. Except during the actual failover of the file server application (usually just a matter of a minute or two), applications and users would not notice any impact of the problem discovery, diagnosis, and solution. The result is better availability and performance because potential problems are detected early and fixed automatically. Resource utilization increases, IT efficiency increases, and administrative cost and time to deployment decrease. Ultimately, the IT utility delivers better value to the enterprise.

VERITAS' Utility Computing Strategy

Many vendors of IT products articulate utility computing strategies for future enterprise information technology. These strategies are sometimes predicated on homogenous solutions using a single common platform. In reality, however, an enterprise hardly ever has the opportunity to start completely anew with information technology. A far more likely scenario is one in which IT utility practices are phased into an IT operation with minimal disruption to existing services. Moreover, a far preferable outcome is a utility strategy that does not entail long-term commitments to a single hardware vendor, but applies utility practices to the most suitable platforms for each application, whatever they may be.

This summarizes VERITAS' utility computing strategy — its goal is to integrate the components that are present in a data center into a unified service delivery infrastructure and, moreover, automate the infrastructure's administration.

The days of homogenous enterprise computing may be over, but the utility computing concept is still sound. As Chapter 1 pointed out, the utility concept is the most efficient way to deliver common services to a large constituency; it is far more efficient than everyone digging his own well or generating his own electrical power.

But in information technology, the opposite often occurs. Lines of business dictate requirements to an IT department, usually including server, storage, software, and other component specifications. The result is silos: multiple "wells" of information technology, providing conceptually identical services in different ways. Utility computing seeks to break this paradigm and provide equivalent services identically to all users, increasing resource utilization and decreasing cost along the way.

Meeting Utility Computing Requirements

Utility computing requires a robust IT infrastructure that includes automatic provisioning of storage, processing, memory, and other resources as needs arise. If an application needs additional resources, they should be configured and provisioned dynamically without impacting service to other users. Since all applications in a utility share the same infrastructure, it must be robust, based on proven technology. Utility computing is "always-on" computing. The goal of VERITAS' utility computing strategy is to enable such an infrastructure that allows an enterprise to create and maintain tiers of standard services that are delivered even when the unexpected happens.

VERITAS enables utility computing by allowing users and integrators to design data centers as computing utilities. VERITAS technology virtualizes heterogeneous components, hiding complexity through abstraction, thereby speeding application deployment while at the same time reducing administrative cost.

All VERITAS technology is available for each of five key platforms (Windows, Solaris, HP-UX, AIX, and Linux) and supports all leading storage devices through leading network components. The VERITAS approach gives IT organizations a common base on which to deploy applications on the most appropriate hardware platforms.

Does the VERITAS utility computing vision relieve pressure on IT executives? It certainly reduces administrative cost and improves resource utilization. It enables faster rollout of services built from standard components. It improves service levels.

Problem solved?

Not quite.

Managing User Perceptions

Utility computing will reduce IT cost and application rollout time and improve system utilization and service levels, but one issue remains. The VERITAS environment described so far does not address the topic of user satisfaction. Users of any service have expectations about how it should behave, and IT is no exception. When a service behaves abnormally, for example, when response is slower than "normal," users complain. But in most cases, complaints are subjective. Users expect "what feels right," based on past experience or other, even more subjective criteria. Without systematic monitoring of service performance and availability, there is no objective way to validate user complaints. Worse yet, in many cases, there are no service-level agreements. Even if performance was measured objectively, users and the IT organization might not agree on "how much is enough."

CommandCentral™ Service

VERITAS addresses user satisfaction with its CommandCentral Service software IT service manager. With CommandCentral Service, IT utility users agree to an expected level of service, and the IT organization agrees to deliver that level of service. CommandCentral Service measures service performance to replace subjective perceptions about whether service levels are being met with objective answers. Measurements of service quality go far in enabling an IT organization to behave as a utility.

A sometimes-surprising result of measuring service levels is users' discovery that service is actually better than specified in the SLA. Complaints about poor performance may be met with the response that performance is still within SLA bounds, that previously, performance had been better than agreed upon. This, too, is a step toward the utility model. Armed with this unpleasant knowledge, users can make business decisions about whether to pay more to be guaranteed the higher level of service. Objective measures and SLAs remove the rancor from this situation, so users and the utility can discuss the business and technical parameters and agree upon changes.

CommandCentral Service software uses a portal model that provisions data protection, clustered application availability, and managed virtual storage. With CommandCentral Service, application managers can select from a menu of standard services, each with an associated cost; IT utility provisions the services to deliver the selected quality of service.

Using CommandCentral Service

When an application is implemented, implementers request service levels through the CommandCentral Service portal. For data protection, for example, desired backup time and frequency, as well as desired recovery time, are selectable. Given a user's selections, CommandCentral Service software recommends the particular technologies to meet them.

For data protection, this might include multiplexed copies, snapshots, higher or lower performance tape drives, and disk-based backup.

Similarly, for online storage provisioning, capacity, rate of expansion, performance, availability, and disaster protection (replication) are all selectable through the CommandCentral Service portal, after which CommandCentral Service software creates virtual devices with the selected characteristics.

With CommandCentral Service, service levels are agreed upon before application deployment. The application manager is told what techniques will be used to meet the specified service level, removing the mystery from service level expectations. The application performance management part of CommandCentral Service collects data for periodic performance reports that reassure users that they are receiving agreed-upon service levels.

CommandCentral Service also makes objective capacity planning a reality. There is great value to both users and to the utility itself in knowing when available storage or server capacity will be consumed and more will be required. Application managers would like to provision additional storage without interruption. IT organizations would like to anticipate usage so that additional storage can be purchased and installed before applications are disrupted. CommandCentral Service gathers data from which resource consumption trends can be deduced and responded to appropriately.

The third component of CommandCentral Service that supports the utility model is billing. In many enterprises, chargeback for IT services is a highly politicized topic, recalling the time of mainframe computing. Users recall that it was the inflexibility and expense of mainframes that provided the impetus for adopting minicomputers, client-server computing, and personal computers, and they don't want to go back. Figure 9-2 illustrates a CommandCentral Service online report on which user chargeback and usage forecasting are displayed.

Many enterprises may never actually charge IT usage back to user departments. Even for these, detailed knowledge of cost at the user level is important because it makes user departments' consumption of IT services visible at the enterprise level. This, in turn, improves alignment of IT with business objectives because it exposes the degree to which IT spending corresponds to business goals. It also improves planning processes. Knowing the potential financial impact of three-way mirroring of all online data or of backup every four hours allows user departments to make business-motivated rather than emotional decisions about the level of IT service they need.

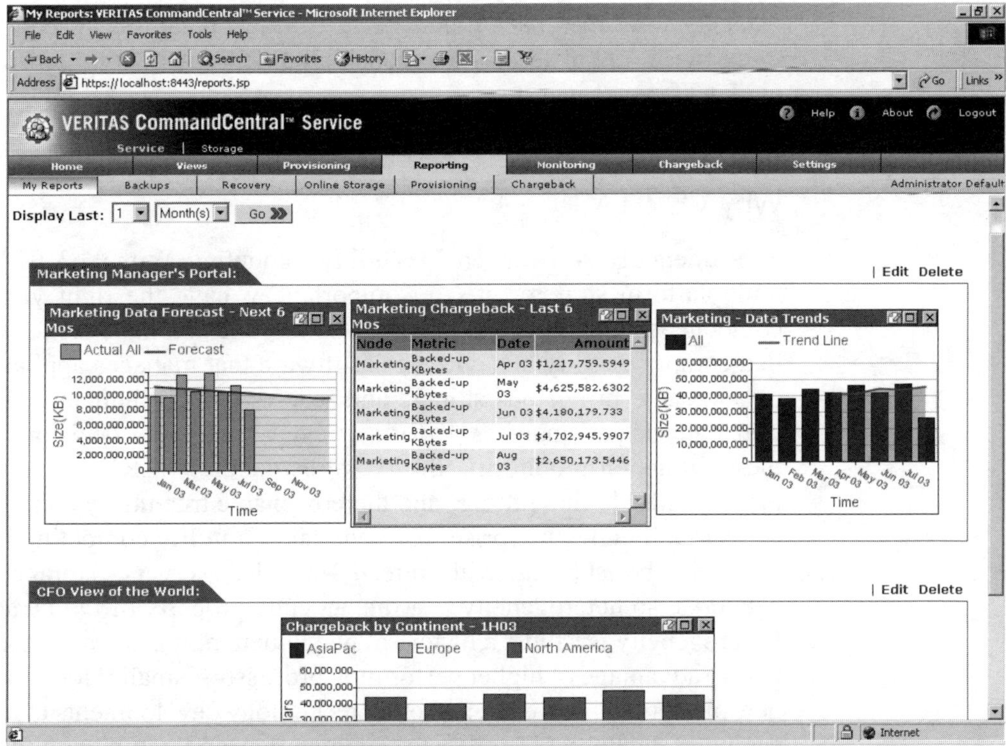

Figure 9-2: VERITAS CommandCentral Service chargeback display

Notebook computers are an instructive example. When a mobile user runs out of notebook storage space, the typical response of a well-managed conventional IT organization is to order a new notebook or disk drive. The user's department might even be billed for the new device. But totally transparent to users (and usually not considered by the IT organization as well) are the hidden costs of the change — the increase in data to back up and in backup times, network bandwidth, and tape media consumption. The costs of ordering, installing, and configuring the hardware, and transferring data from the old computer or disk to the new are all real to the IT organization, but they are transparent to the user and very often not even accounted for by the IT organization.

If user departments received even a notional bill for these hidden services, they might give consideration to whether absolutely everything on a notebook's disk is essential. Without motivation to conserve, the answer is, "of course everything should stay online because there is no incremental cost, because carefully managing notebook disk contents consumes user time." With full accountability, users might think twice and at least make considered decisions about consuming hidden IT services.

Why VERITAS

Fundamentally, software enables utility computing. With the VERITAS multiplatform strategy, it's not important to have the right vendor's components. It's important to integrate them and automate the functions that comprise utility behavior. It is software that manages applications dynamically, provisions storage and servers without human intervention, collects and analyzes performance data, and bases decisions to do these things on monitoring the IT infrastructure. VERITAS software technologies do these things and thereby enable true utility computing.

Virtually any enterprise that undertakes a utility computing initiative will be starting with already-installed servers, storage, and networks, so heterogeneity is a fundamental property of the IT utility. Heterogeneity isn't just a historical phenomenon; it is always desirable to take advantage of higher performing processors, smaller form factors, new platforms like Linux, and other technology developments to reduce capital costs. For an IT utility to minimize cost and optimize services, it must have utility software for all the platforms that it supports.

Finally, VERITAS has a long history of delivering robust technology for the most critical functions in the data center. These three factors — a software-centric outlook, inherent heterogeneity, and a strong history — are the keys to becoming a successful utility computing supplier. VERITAS delivers the storage, clustering, and network software building blocks that enable IT organizations to implement the utility model, improving utilization and quality of service without disrupting enterprise business.

Chapter Summary

- Information technology executives are faced with pressures from threc quarters: executive management wants lower IT costs, users want more services, and technology is increasing the complexity of the environment. Utility computing offers relief from these pressures.
- Through a combination of technology acquisitions and integration of existing technologies, VERITAS is positioning itself to be the premier supplier of utility computing software for all major platforms.
- The primary VERITAS enabling technologies for utility computing are storage virtualization, application availability management, application performance management, storage resource management, automated server provisioning, and workflow management. The company offers products in all of these areas, and is currently engaged in integrating these offerings more closely to provide even better utility computing facilities.
- In addition to the basic facilities that manipulate IT resources to better satisfy user demands and meet service-level agreements, VERITAS has introduced its CommandCentral Service portal to automate the definition and tracking of service-level agreements between users and an IT utility. By making service-level agreements explicit and precise and reporting on performance against them, CommandCentral Service software removes much of the basis for user dissatisfaction with utility computing before it occurs.
- VERITAS' utility computing strategy is inherently software-based and multiplatform, making it practical for enterprises to evolve to the utility model with a minimum of disruption of existing services and displacement of equipment.

AFTERWORD

So You Want an IT Utility

"Once the toothpaste is out of the tube, it's hard to get it back in."

— H.R. Haldeman

The benefits of utility computing seem obvious: The enterprise benefits by saving money, users benefit with increased service levels, and vendors get to license software for small projects of brief duration as well as large, ongoing ones. Utility computing should be a "win" for everyone, even if it will take some time to realize its full promise. The ideal IT utility will have one unified network rather than several disjointed ones, one storage pool rather than hundreds of disk arrays, one computing fabric rather than hundreds of unrelated servers, and one application integration mechanism instead of a unique mechanism for each application. While not all of this can be delivered today, remarkable progress has been made even in the last two years.

Today, in 2004, it is fair to say that the base technologies for delivering a utility computing infrastructure exist, and the major challenge faced by vendors is in integrating them. From a technology standpoint, abstraction, virtualization, and automation are the keys to success. Today, abstraction is moving from the realm of vendor-specific APIs in the direction of standards,[21] virtualization is essentially a solved problem to which finishing touches are being applied, and automation is making great strides, as outlined in Chapter 9. As Chapter 9 also points out, the greatest challenge that vendors face today is tying all the pieces together, so, for example, when monitoring software detects a problem and root cause analysis software determines the cause, additional

21. As the initiator of the SNIA's Storage Management Interface Standard (SMI-S), VERITAS is in the forefront of data center management standardization activities. Additional activities similar to the SMI-S are to be expected in the future.

resources can be configured and provisioned, and workload readjusted, all without human intervention. This is the "holy grail" of utility computing infrastructure toward which all vendors are striving in some form.

But what about users? Are there requirements that enterprises must meet in order to make utility computing successful?

The answer, of course, is yes. For utility computing to succeed, first and foremost, attitudes throughout the enterprise must change. People must "get it" — they must stop thinking about IT as computers and disks and tape drives and start thinking in terms of virtualized services and the service-level agreements that accompany them. Nobody thinks about how water gets to the tap or how electricity gets to the outlet. They are basic services delivered by utilities; the infrastructure that makes them happen is taken for granted. Users and IT organizations alike must begin thinking of applications as consumers of storage, computing, and other services provided by the IT utility and worry less (eventually not at all) about implementation technologies.

In the same way that consumers pay for consumption of utility services without thinking twice about it, IT users must begin to think in terms of the cost of the IT services that they consume and in terms of tiered pricing based on service quality. Utility IT is just another cost of doing business, like electricity or office space, about which business-based decisions can be made. Once a business unit determines that a particular level of service is necessary, how that level is achieved should not be of concern. The business should be content with regular and demand-based reports that summarize what it is consuming and how much it is costing the enterprise.

Software is a key enabler of utility computing, and users have a role there as well. Application developers and managers must be trained in the use of utility services and in taking an active part in managing their IT service consumption.

Finally, a successful conversion to utility computing requires a partnership between users and the IT organization, with both parties playing active roles. The active roles begin with a careful baseline analysis of the enterprise and its applications, as Chapter 5 describes. The IT organization contributes technology and operational expertise to this baseline; just as importantly, users contribute business knowledge and experience. Together, the two determine which services are most crucial and which applications would most benefit from utility computing. Following the baseline and the resulting decision to implement an IT utility, new processes must be defined for deploying new applications in the utility context.

Today, IT utility design and implementation skills are rarely found in end-user enterprises. Engaging consultants to help guide the analysis and development phases and impart their skills for future self-sufficiency will be an important success factor in many cases. Consulting organizations (including VERITAS) offer a variety of well-defined services such as operational efficiency assessment, scorecard development (as described in Chapter 5), architectural blueprinting, and service definition that can simplify utility definition implementation and increase the probability of success. In the early stages, consultants can also help make objective decisions about standard hardware and software components and can often see commonalities among the requirements of existing applications, precisely because they are removed from the situation. Finally, as parties who do this full time, they are likely to be aware of tools and trends that would be expensive and difficult for the enterprise to discover on its own. While the ultimate goal should always be enterprise self-sufficiency, experienced consultants can be extraordinarily useful in "jump starting" a move to utility computing.

As the new millennium begins, technology has made possible a new architecture for providing IT services to the enterprise. The new architecture benefits all concerned — users, IT providers, and enterprises as a whole. In the words of an international automaker, "It's worth a look."

Appendixes

APPENDIX A

An Open Architectural Framework

The International Standards Organization (ISO) standard *Reference Model for Open Distributed Processing* (RM-ODP) defines a reference model for developing distributed system architectures. The RM-ODP might be thought of as a meta-standard, or framework of architectural concepts and terminology, which facilitates development of utility computing standards. This chapter introduces the RM-ODP and illustrates some aspects of its use in creating architectural models for utility computing.[22]

The RM-ODP

The RM-ODP incorporates five viewpoints that project onto a distributed computer system. The viewpoints represent the interests of stakeholders in a system — the builders, owners, users, maintainers, and so forth. Taken together, the viewpoints are a complete architecture. Because stakeholders' interests peak at different times, the viewpoints also provide an excellent picture of a system's life cycle. Figure A-1 illustrates the five RM-ODP viewpoints as they apply to utility computing and also underscores the point that a computing utility exists within an environment that constrains its behavior.

22. The book *Architecting with RM-ODP* by Janis Putman (Prentice Hall, 2001) ISBN 0130191167 describes the RM-ODP in detail.

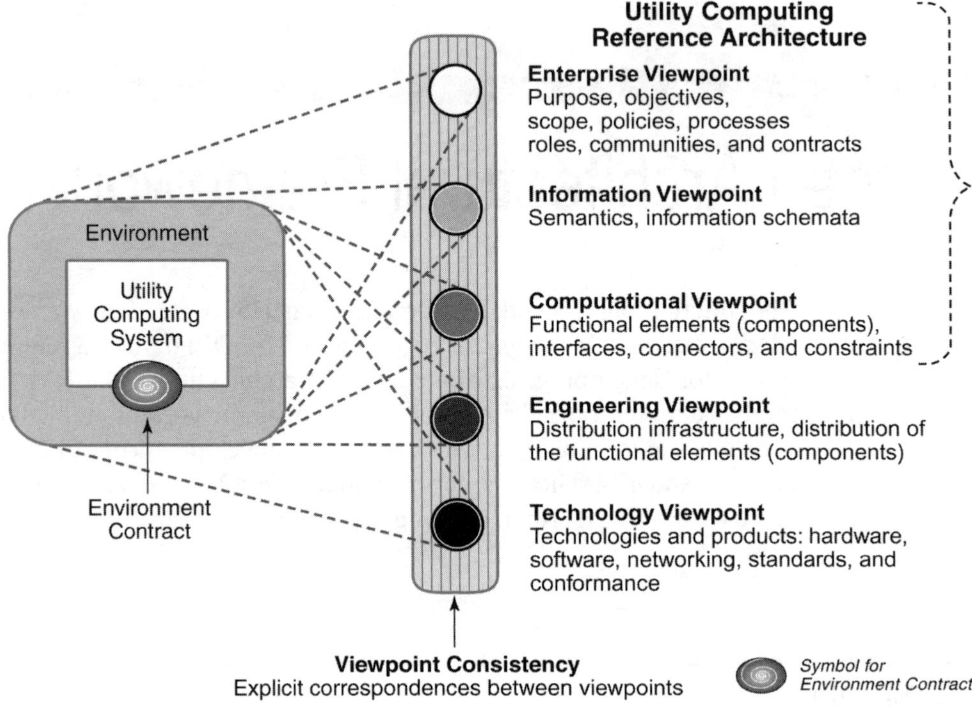

Figure A-1: Using the RM-ODP reference framework to model a computing utility

The five viewpoints are:

- ***Enterprise***. This is the viewpoint of a utility's owners (executive management) and users. It defines a utility's role within the enterprise, including its scope, policies, communities, contracts, and relationship with its environment. This viewpoint also defines the sources of data managed by the utility.
- ***Information***. This is the viewpoint of information officers, database administrators, and other individuals who manage enterprise information resources. It defines information elements and their flow around the enterprise, as well as processes for manipulating them.
- ***Computational***. This is the viewpoint of application architects. It defines the utility's computational objects (roughly: applications) and interfaces between them. This viewpoint defines environment contracts that state what applications and the utility should expect of each other. It does not define physical distribution of objects among processors.

- ***Engineering***. This is the viewpoint of system designers and platform engineers. It defines the utility's information distribution infrastructure (network), the configuration of its computers and their relationships to computational objects. This viewpoint describes how business applications use the utility's services.
- ***Technology***. This is the viewpoint of application implementers. It defines specific hardware, software, and networking technologies and where they are used within the utility, as well as technical standards and reference points for testing implementations against specifications.

One important purpose of the different RM-ODP viewpoints is to highlight how different stakeholders view common and related elements. For example, the enterprise viewpoint might identify what data a utility will manage, whereas the information viewpoint would define schemas, and the technology viewpoint would identify the database management products to be used. Architects using the RM-ODP define explicit relationships between related elements in different viewpoints so that viewpoints remain consistent as changes occur in the course of development. Viewpoints remain consistent because the explicit relationships between elements make it obvious when a change in one viewpoint should propagate to related elements in others.

Among the RM-ODP IT utility viewpoints illustrated in Figure A-1, the enterprise, information, and computational viewpoints specify *what* the utility does. They are independent of the engineering and technology viewpoints that specify how the utility accomplishes its job. Taken together, the three constitute a reference architecture for an IT utility that is independent of the applications (users) that it serves and the implementation technologies. The reference architecture is not constrained by engineering or technology limitations. Using an architectural reference model, business and technical analysts can explore the business and financial consequences of policy changes and propagate them into the engineering and technology viewpoints to estimate costs and other impacts. The enterprise, information, computational, and engineering viewpoints are independent of the technology choices for a utility.

Objects

The RM-ODP is an object-based model. As is typical with object-based systems, an RM-ODP object is an abstraction that can represent anything that can be defined by a state (parameters that take on values) and behavior (specified responses to well-defined stimuli). Objects encapsulate (hide) much of the detail of the things they represent. They expose only the externally visible state and behavior prompted by external inputs. Objects are useful for modeling both business and computer systems.

Objects can model components, systems, or even human beings. They are hierarchical; an object may contain other objects (e.g., a data center object may contain several computer objects). An object can be as large as the entire computing utility or as small as a single application or hardware component. Obviously, different types of objects are useful in different viewpoints.

By specifying objects in more or less detail, models with different levels of precision, completeness, and formality can be constructed. High-level RM-ODP models representing each viewpoint can be useful to executives, but they can also be refined to a level of detail from which a programmer can develop code, or indeed, a computer program can translate them into code or actions without human assistance.

Utilities and the RM-ODP

To help understand the key aspects of the RM-ODP-based reference framework as they apply to IT utilities, this section compares the delivery of electrical power by a utility company with the delivery of IT services by a computing utility, using architectures based on the RM-ODP framework in both cases.

The Electrical Utility

Figure A-2 diagrams a heating system (a user) that uses electricity (the commodity) delivered by an electric company (a utility). Electricity heats water, which flows to the radiator (an application), which gives off heat (a business purpose). A thermostat detects falling room temperature (monitoring) and signals the boiler to supply more heat (a service request). The utility meets the demand for more electricity transparently to the user. If the room occupant (management) decides that the thermostat setting is too high or too low (the demand), the thermostat can be adjusted, causing electricity usage (and therefore the bill) to rise or fall.

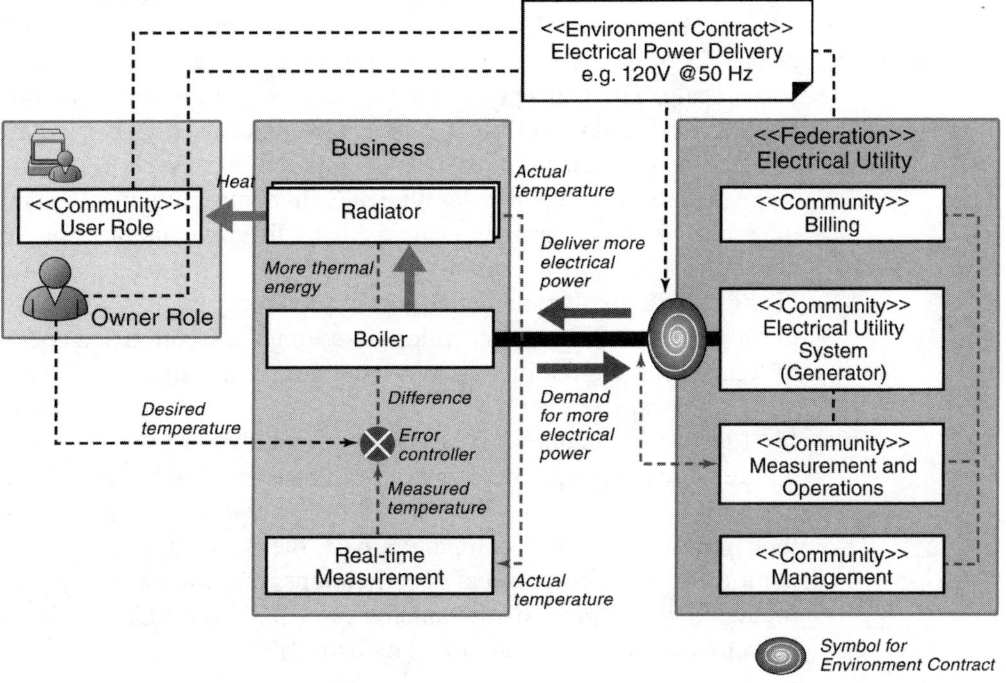

Figure A-2: A heating system (user) connected to an electric company (utility)

There is a (probably implicit) service-level agreement (SLA) between this utility and its users (labeled "Environment Contract" in the figure, for reasons discussed later in the appendix). For example, the company supplies electricity at a standard voltage level and current frequency, up to a power level agreed upon in advance. Electricity flows through a meter that records consumption data used to compute users' charges.

The management of the heating system (application) buys a commodity (electricity) to help it serve a business purpose (keeping people warm). If the utility can supply electricity to many heating systems (and televisions and toasters and other applications) more reliably and less expensively than what is supplied by private generators, it will be successful.

The users in this example are part of a community consisting of all the homes and businesses served by a generating plant. This community is *federated* — its members are independent of each other for most purposes but cooperate at some level to maintain reliable electrical service for everyone. The generating plant may also be part of a larger federated community — typically all of an electric company's plants are interconnected and can redirect power to where it is needed. There is also a federation of electric companies, somewhat similar to the Grid discussed in Chapter 4, that share resources dynamically on an even larger scale. The concept of user federations and the rules that govern them is important to a utility's architecture, since users of particular services are in essence federations with common interests.

A federation is a particular type of ODP community in which multiple groups that are normally responsible to different authorities agree to cooperate to achieve a specific objective. Because implementation of an IT utility will involve many mergers of separately managed subsystems to support common interests, rules governing the creation and operation of federations and the interactions among them are an important part of an IT utility specification.

Electric companies have policies that constrain the environment within which they operate. For example, users are not permitted to tamper with meters and may be obliged to allow meter readers access to their premises. For the company's part, the power it distributes must conform to certain technical specifications, and the company may be regulated with regard to how much it can charge for different classes of power usage (e.g., consumer and industrial).

The Computing Utility

Figure A-3 diagrams a business function (a user[23]) that consumes computing and storage (commodities) delivered by a data center (a utility). Computers run programs that process data (applications) to record sales or serve customers (a business purpose). Measurement tools detect rising response time (monitoring) and signal the management console to supply more computing power (a service request). Ideally, the utility meets the demand transparently to the user. If the business unit (management) decides that more users must be serviced faster (the demand), resources can be added or removed, causing usage (and therefore the bill) to rise or fall.

23. To an IT utility, a user is the entity that consumes the commodities it delivers. Thus, if an IT utility delivers online storage, backup, and computing services, its users are business applications. Typically, a user of an IT utility is not a human being but a business application. Typically too, business applications serve human users.

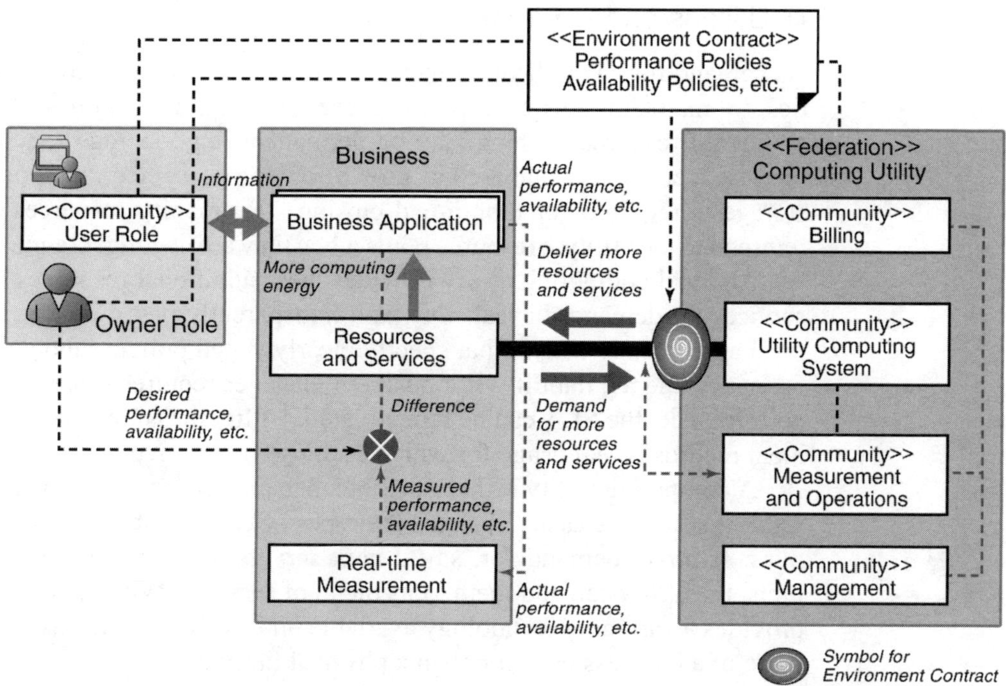

Figure A-3: A business application (user) connected to a computing utility

The management of the business function buys commodities (processing and storage) to help it serve a business purpose (processing data). If the utility can supply these commodities to many business units (and operating departments) more reliably and less expensively than departmental computers supply them, it will be successful.

Like an electrical company, an IT utility also observes permissions, obligations, and prohibitions that constrain its actions and those of its users in the operational environment. For example, executive management might require that a utility offer 99.999 percent available computing and online storage services, even though they are not strictly economical. For their part, users might be constrained by mandatory security measures or by prohibitions against storing MP3 or JPG files on utility storage resources.

IT Utilities and Demand

As demand for an application increases, it requires more IT commodities to maintain adequate performance. The utility supplies these additional resources, which may be permanent (e.g., storage required because a customer database has grown) or temporary (e.g., temporary storage is required for month-end closing). Temporary resources are returned to the utility's resource pools when they are no longer required.

An ideal computing utility provides these additional resources and services on-demand, in real time, and transparently based on service-level agreements (SLAs) that specify clearly stated policies about performance and availability. If a business manager requires more or less performance, the SLA can be renegotiated. Utility measurement equipment records actual usage for which each user is charged.

A computing utility is more flexible than an electric company in the sense that it more easily changes the types of commodities that it supplies. If broad demand for, say, Linux servers arises in the business units, the utility can add them to its menu of services. Whether or not it provides a particular technology available on its distribution network is more of a business question than a physical limitation.

Both of these examples are modeled using the concepts and, to a limited extent, the terminology of the RM-ODP. The role of the RM-ODP is to abstract the essentials of what is being modeled as objects, each of which plays a role in the model. For example, an IT utility would normally have an object playing a resource-provisioning role. The role might be played by a human object or, in a more advanced utility, by an automated software object. Thinking in terms of objects rather than people or software modules tends to create more flexible, evolvable utility architectures.

Typical IT Utility Roles

To illustrate the RM-ODP concept of roles, Figure A-4 shows some of the most common roles found in an IT utility — resource manager, resource coordinator, and service manager. Each role consists of a set of functions, which might be performed by different objects at different times. For example, automated tools might perform the discovery, monitoring, and reporting functions of the *storage* resource manager role, whereas provisioning, virtualization, change management, and upgrade might require intervention by a human object. Identifying roles and the functions that comprise them in this way clarifies the impact of changes in a utility. For example, installing an automatic provisioning tool would shift that function from a human object to a software one. The human would be freed — most likely to perform the remaining functions for more objects (e.g., manage more storage or computers).

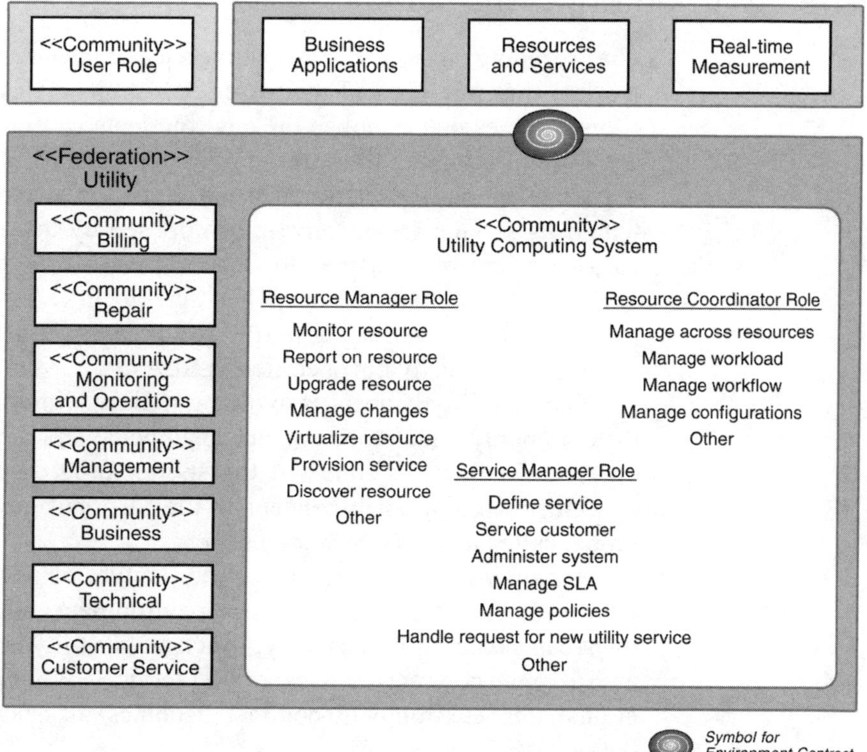

Figure A-4: Roles and functions in a computing utility

Identifying roles also makes the interactions between them obvious. For example, the resource coordinator role in Figure A-4 would be responsible for managing multiple types of resources and allocating them to users. This role would be responsible for delivering more processing power or other resources to applications that request it, using services of individual resource manager roles. In some utilities, this role might be associated with a human. As more sophisticated tools become available, certain functions could be transferred to software components, again increasing the scope of the human to perform remaining functions. Maintaining clear delineations between roles (for example, between the roles of resource manager and resource coordinator) makes it unlikely that critical functions will be neglected when a utility makes technology changes (e.g., installing software to automate resource provisioning).

The Environment Contract

The preceding discussion alludes to service-level agreements and also to the fact that utilities and their users constrain themselves to observe common rules that establish the environments within which they operate. For traditional utilities, these rules are sometimes legal constraints (e.g., a telephone company must make service available to all homes within its service area), sometimes imposed by the utility (e.g., cable customers are not allowed to connect amplifiers to their incoming cable), and sometimes by unspoken agreement (e.g., ISP users refrain from generating spam). These rules of common behavior are assumed — they are typically not specified in SLAs.

The IT utility concept is evolving rapidly without having many of the commonly understood and accepted behaviors required for smooth operation in place. To cope with this shortcoming, the RM-ODP defines an agreement similar in concept to the SLA but greatly expanded in scope, called an *environment contract.*

An environment contract may be thought of as a specification of what an IT utility can expect from its environment and what the environment can expect from the utility. When an IT utility is first designed, an environment contract defines required services. When the utility is operational, the environment contract becomes the standard for service delivery.

An environment contract specifies both communications and semantics. From a communication standpoint, it specifies:

- Protocols used to transfer data (e.g., TCP/IP, iSCSI, Fibre Channel, tar tape)
- Data representation (e.g., database and file formats for interchangeability)
- Communication between the utility and its environment (e.g., workflow systems)

The semantic specifications include rules, policies, security domains, and environment constraints. For example, external interactions might have to pass through a firewall, while internal ones might be "inside the firewall."

Figure A-5 lists the parameters of a complete environment contract. The quality of service specifications typical of today's SLA are shown within the larger context of the environment contract. A mature utility should have an environment contract for each business application to which it provides services and for each service it provides.

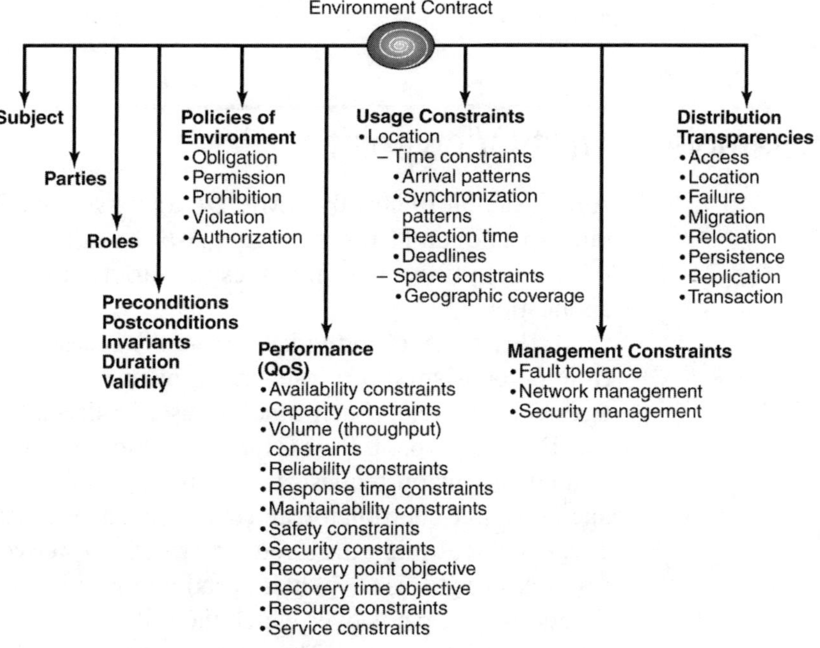

Figure A-5: Components of an environment contract

An IT utility's environment contracts should reflect the cost of providing services. Charging more for a higher quality of service (e.g., for mirrored storage or hourly backups) is a familiar notion. But as Figure A-5 suggests, other, less obvious aspects of utility services may be costly to provide as well. For example, provisioning additional online storage within minutes or hours of a user request clearly costs the utility more than provisioning with a week's notice, and this should be reflected in the price of service.

By associating quality of service with cost, a utility is able to provide affordable flexibility. Operators can use resource utilization data to adjust operational policies for optimal effect. Some IT organizations may bill users for resource consumption, while others may simply use the knowledge to guide business decisions.

A mature IT utility should have environment contract templates expressed in users' terms. Utility users should not have to be experts in the technologies used to implement services, for example. Careful coordination of environment contracts with user communities enables a computing utility to respond gracefully to changing usage patterns and business needs and sets the stage for automation as tools become available.

A Sample IT Utility Viewpoint

As an example of how the RM-ODP framework can be used to represent one aspect of an IT utility, Figure A-6 shows an engineering viewpoint of an IT utility that provides a variety of services to business applications.

In Figure A-6, individuals (role A) access a business application (role B) consisting of presentation, business logic, and database management functions. Each function uses utility services, represented as role D through role I. Role C manages resources and provisions services to applications on request. It incorporates the workflow, service manager, resource coordinator, and resource manager roles. These managers create services (e.g., mirrored storage (E) or network access (F)) from resources (e.g., disks, switch ports) and provision them to application functions. The paths over which the utility provides services are called channels in the figure. The channel represents the utility's ability to measure usage, both for billing and for evaluating the level of service actually provided against the SLA component of the environment contract.

As an engineering viewpoint, Figure A-6 represents roles and functions, not the specific types of computers that execute them or the specific interconnects and protocols that link them (those would be represented in a technology viewpoint). Identifying roles and functions in the abstract makes it easy to analyze the impact of proposed changes throughout the utility. For example, replacing a human storage service manager with automatic provisioning software would require that business application functions that use storage services be able to interact with the software and the software be capable of controlling storage devices of whatever sort are present in the utility.

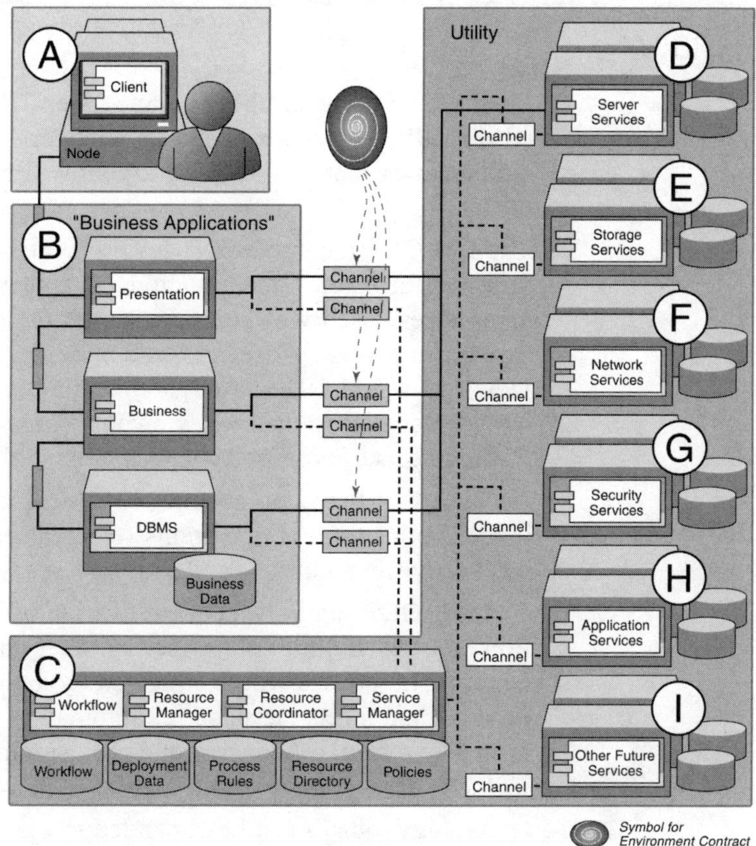

Figure A-6: Engineering viewpoint of an IT utility

Lack of automation has historically been a barrier to implementation of true IT utilities. Services can be standardized, but without automation, running the utility is labor intensive and therefore expensive and unreliable. Automatic discovery, configuration, provisioning, and reclaiming of resources is a major area of computer system management research and development.

Some users are uncomfortable with the idea that their data, applications, and services may share physical resources with those of another organization. Even where technology supports resource sharing, security and operational considerations must be addressed, and users must be persuaded that the benefits outweigh the risks.

Summary

- The ISO Reference Model for Open Distributed Processing (RM-ODP) defines a reference framework for distributed system architectures that can be used to define the architecture of an IT utility.
- The RM-ODP incorporates five viewpoints, which represent enterprise, information, computation, engineering, and technology approaches. Each viewpoint represents the interests of a different constituency (e.g., executives tend to be interested in the enterprise view). An RM-ODP-based architecture describes relationships between objects in different viewpoints, making it easy to analyze ripple effects of proposed changes in the utility.
- Because it is based on abstract objects, RM-ODP can be used to model both business operations (e.g., a heating system that uses electricity from a utility) and IT utility operations.
- The RM-ODP suggests the identification of roles that specify functional responsibilities. Abstracting roles and functions has two benefits. It clarifies what is affected by a change in technology or process, and it sets the stage for automation of routine utility functions like resource discovery and provisioning.
- For a utility to succeed, the SLA that is common in information technology today must be expanded into an environment contract that is similar to but more comprehensive than the SLA.
- A sample of an RM-ODP-based architecture for an IT utility illustrates the importance of roles and viewpoints.
- An enterprise planning to implement an IT utility should become knowledgeable about the RM-ODP and seriously consider using it to create an IT utility architecture before making expensive financial commitments.

APPENDIX B

Utility Computing Planning Forms

The forms that follow are designed to be used to collect information and develop plans for implementing a utility computing environment. They are, however, just examples, as are the data in the tables. Different environments will need to alter them to properly fit their environments. The data collected here will enable you to build a plan to migrate from a traditional computing environment to utility computing. Careful form design is important; all required information should be collected in one pass. Continually returning to customers to request more information will not make the IT utility popular. In many cases the answer to a question will be "no" or "not known." Answers such as these are just as valid as any more detailed answer.

Baselining

Application Name	Department	Business Criticality (1-5)	Availability (1-5)	Standard Services Used	Metered Usage	Downtime Cost Per Hour
e.g., SAP R3	Finance	1	1	Backup, storage provisioning, server provisioning, client provisioning, and rollout	No	$2M

Business Criticality terms should be defined specifically for each enterprise. For example:

- 1 – Critical (e.g., online shop, CRM)
- 2 – Near critical (e.g., e-mail, order processing)
- 3 – Medium criticality (e.g., file and print serving)
- 4 – Not critical (e.g., payroll)
- 5 – Redundant (reporting that was useful five years ago)

Availability terms should be defined specifically for each enterprise. For example:

- 1 – Highest (e.g., replicated data, wide-area failover, clustered, tape backup)
- 2 – High (e.g., local cluster, tape backup)
- 3 – Medium (e.g., daily tape backup)
- 4 – Low (e.g., back up once a week)
- 5 – Lowest (e.g., not even backed up)

User Department View

Department:				
IT Service Required	**Dependent**	**Taken for Granted or Planned?**	**Current Implementation: Enabler or Inhibitor**	**Deficiencies**
e.g., backup	Yes	Taken for granted	Enabler	Slow to add new servers

IT View

Service	Depts. Serviced	OSs Supported	One-off?	Financial Metrics?	Performance Metrics?	Accountable?	Chargeback?
e.g., backup	All	All (Windows, Solaris, HP/UX, AIX, Linux, etc.)	No	No	Yes (limited)	No	No
e.g., DB2	Finance	AIX	Yes	No	No	No	No

IT Technology Support

Department	# Servers	# OSs used	# Storage/ # Storage Types	# Applications or # App Types	# Networks
e.g., Finance	20	3 AIX, 10 Solaris, 7 Windows	Not clear, some EMC, some IBM, some Sun	1 SAP, 3 Oracle, 1 DB2, …	2 CISCO

IT Planning

Service	Score	Utility/Factory/ Consultancy/ Operation	Availability Expectations	Performance Expectations	Growth Expectations	IT Cost Growth	Org. Structure
e.g., backup	1	Utility	24x7	SLA / backup window restrictions	50 percent year on year	???	Centralized management by IT department, local users enabled for restore

Glossary of IT Utility Terminology

This glossary defines terminology as it is used in this book. The authors have created some of the definitions, while others are reproduced by permission from an online dictionary maintained by the Storage Networking Industry Association (SNIA), whose contribution is gratefully acknowledged. The definitions contributed by the SNIA are reproduced without alteration, and identify the SNIA as their source. The online dictionary from which they are drawn can be found at http://www.snia.org/dictionary. The SNIA updates it regularly as technology and usage evolve. Definitions that are not identified as SNIA contributions are the work of the authors and the lexicographer.

administrator
A person charged with the installation, configuration, and management of a computer system, network, storage subsystem, database, or application. (SNIA)

Advanced Research Projects Agency (ARPA)
Formerly the U.S. government's research agency for space and strategic missile research. In 1958, with the formation of NASA, the activities of ARPA began to focus mainly on computer science and information processing. One of ARPA's goals was to enable computers at universities around the country to communicate using a common protocol.

agent
A software component that provides an interface between a client and the services of a server. Agents are generally used to enable interoperation between clients and servers that were not designed to be aware of each other.

alert
An alarm or notification of an event.

ARPA
See Advanced Research Projects Agency.

ARPAnet
The Advanced Research Projects Agency Network of the U.S. Department of Defense is the predecessor of the global Internet.

assisted management
A stage in an enterprise's transition from conventional data processing to the IT utility model during which an enterprise first starts to act like a utility. Routine tasks are either fully automated or follow a strict process workflow. Component-level SLAs are executed. Benefits at this stage include greater operational efficiency and accountability.

authentication
CONTEXT [Network] The process of determining what principal a requestor or provider of services is or represents. **CONTEXT [Security]** A security measure designed to establish the validity of a transmission, message, or originator, or a means of verifying an individual's authorization to receive information. (SNIA)

authorization
CONTEXT [Network] The process of determining that a requestor is allowed to receive a service or perform an operation. Access control is an example of authorization. **CONTEXT [Security]** The limiting of usage of information system resources to authorized users, programs, processes or other systems. Access control is a specific type of authorization. Authorization is formally described as controlling usage by subjects of objects. (SNIA)

automated provisioning
The dynamic increase or decrease of resources allocated to a user or application without human intervention.

autonomic computing initiative
An IBM initiative to create a self-managing IT infrastructure in which self-configuring, self-healing, self-optimizing, and self-protecting servers, network components, and applications operate as a unit.

availability

The amount of time that a system is available during those time periods when it is expected to be available. Availability is often measured as a percentage of an elapsed year. For example, 99.95% availability equates to 4.38 hours of downtime in a year (0.0005 * 365 * 24 = 4.38) for a system that is expected to be available all the time. *cf.* **data availability**, **high availability** (SNIA)

B

backup client

A computer system that controls data that must be backed up by and restored from a separate backup server.

backup server

A computer system that performs backups and restores for other computer systems, receiving the data to be backed up over an enterprise or storage network.

backup window

The period of time during which backups are or are permitted to be taken.

broadband

Any of several digital technologies that provide consumers with some or all of voice, high-speed data, and video services.

C

CATV

Acronym for community area television. Also known as cable TV.

CERN
Organisation Européenne pour la Recherche Nucléaire (European Laboratory for Nuclear Research), a research laboratory headquartered in Geneva, Switzerland, and funded by many different countries. While most of their work deals with nuclear physics, the CERN is known for Tim Berners-Lee's pioneering work in developing the World Wide Web portion of the Internet.

change control
Comprehensive control over changes made to information technology systems or components. Change control includes precise written description, authorization, and records of request and execution.

chargeback
The process of billing an internal user for use of the enterprise's resources.

client-server (architecture)
An architecture for distributed computer systems in which some computers (the servers) deliver services to other computers (the clients) over a network. File and database access are the two most common uses of client-server architecture.

cluster
A collection of computers that are interconnected (typically at high speeds) for the purpose of improving reliability, availability, serviceability and/or performance (via load balancing). Often, clustered computers have access to a common pool of storage and run special software to coordinate the component computers' activities. (SNIA)

clustering
Use of a cluster to solve data processing problems.

cluster manager
A software component that manages interactions among the servers in a cluster. A cluster manager is responsible for monitoring resource and application status and conducting failover according to predefined policies.

connectivity
The set of devices with which a given program or device can communicate.

D

data availability
The amount of time that a data is accessible by applications during those time periods when it is expected to be available. Data availability is often measured as a percentage of an elapsed year. For example, 99.95% availability equates to 4.38 hours of unavailability in a year (0.0005 * 365 * 24 = 4.38) for a set of data that is expected to be available all the time. *cf.* **availability**, **high availability**. (SNIA)

data replication
The process of maintaining two or more identical sets of data by copying updates to a primary set to secondary datasets across a network (usually IP) as the updates made occur. Databases, files, or virtual block storage device contents can be replicated. Replication can be synchronous, with updates being copied in lockstep, or asynchronous, with copying allowed to lag by a bounded amount.

data sharing
Coordinated simultaneous access to data by two or more clients. Disks, virtual block storage devices, file systems, and files may all be shared by multiple applications running on the same or different application servers. Data sharing requires coordination of client accesses to preserve data correctness when multiple clients read or update data simultaneously.

database manager
Synonym for database management system (DBMS). A suite of data management software that organizes data independently of applications, imposes syntactic and semantic constraints on it, and maintains transactional integrity.

DBMS
See database manager.

deployment
The process of placing IT resources into service.

Digital Subscriber Link (DSL)
A technology for making high-bandwidth Internet access available to homes and small businesses over ordinary telephone lines.

downtime
See recovery time.

DSL
See Digital Subscriber Link.

duty cycle
The percentage of time during which a system is actively performing its function. A system that serves users for eight hours a day during five workdays per week has a duty cycle of 23.8 percent (40 of 168 hours).

environment contract
A formal specification of what an IT utility can expect from its environment and what the environment can expect from the utility.

Ethernet
The predominant local area networking technology, based on packetized transmissions between physical ports over a variety of electrical and optical media. Ethernet can transport any of several upper layer protocols, the most popular of which is TCP/IP. Ethernet standards are maintained by the IEEE 802.3 committee. (SNIA)

event
An action or occurrence detected by a computer program. Events can be human actions, such as mouse clicks or keystrokes, or system occurrences, such as memory exhaustion or disk drive failure.

event console
A central location to which events in a distributed system are reported. An event console typically has a user interface so that events can be signaled to humans interactively.

failover
The automatic substitution of a functionally equivalent system component for a failed one. The term failover is most often applied to intelligent controllers connected to the same storage devices and host computers. If one of the controllers fails, failover occurs, and the survivor takes over its I/O load. (SNIA)

failover cluster
A cluster whose sole purpose is to increase application availability by failing applications over from one server to another.

failover management software (FMS)
Software that enables failover within a cluster by checking the health of cluster members and directing resources to failover from one cluster member to another, as needed to ensure application availability.

failure
A malfunction of a system or a component in a system that impedes the system from performing its intended function or renders it unable to perform entirely.

fault
Synonym for failure.

fault management software
A suite of computer programs that detect, report, and analyze faults in a distributed computer system.

Fibre Channel
A set of standards for a serial I/O bus capable of transferring data between two ports at up to 100 MBytes/second, with standards proposals to go to higher speeds. Fibre Channel supports point to point, arbitrated loop, and switched topologies. Fibre Channel was completely developed through industry cooperation, unlike SCSI, which was developed by a vendor and submitted for standardization after the fact. (SNIA)

file system
(1) A suite of software programs that collectively implement a file abstraction for computer system applications.
(2) A virtual storage device that has been formatted by file system software to store and retrieve files.

FMS
See failover management software.

full backup
A backup copy that contains a copy of all the data in the designated file set, such as a file system or database.

HBA
See host bus adapter.

heterogeneity
An architectural or physical difference between two IT components that prevents them from being commonly used or managed. Heterogeneity is encountered in operating systems, block storage devices, storage interconnects, disk drives, and other components.

hierarchical storage management (HSM)

A technique for managing online storage occupied by large numbers of files by moving seldom-accessed files to secondary storage and reclaiming their primary storage space for other use. Hierarchical storage management moves, or *migrates*, files in such a way that they can be recalled transparently (as if they were still in their original locations) when applications access them.

high availability

The ability of a system to perform its function continuously (without interruption) for a significantly longer period of time than the reliabilities of its individual components would suggest. High availability is most often achieved through failure tolerance. High availability is not an easily quantifiable term. Both the bounds of a system that is called highly available and the degree to which its availability is extraordinary must be clearly understood on a case-by-case basis. (SNIA)

host bus adapter (HBA)

A device that provides an interface between a computer's internal I/O bus and an external I/O bus or storage network.

HSM

See hierarchical storage management.

HTTP

See HyperText Transfer Protocol.

HVAC

Acronym for heating, ventilating, air conditioning.

hypertext

Computer readable text in which cross-reference links (hyperlinks) have been inserted, enabling the user to call up relevant data from other files, or parts of the same file, by clicking on a coded word or symbol.

HyperText Transfer Protocol (HTTP)

An application level protocol, usually run over TCP/IP, that enables the exchange of files via the World Wide Web. (SNIA)

I

ICMP
See Internet Control Message Protocol.

incident
A detailed record of one or more correlated events that require response in some form.

incremental backup
A form of backup in which only data objects that have changed since some prior backup are copied. Individual data objects can be restored from incremental backups, but restoring an entire file system or database requires both a baseline full backup and a complete sequence of incremental backups.

information processing/information processing service
See information service.

information service
A computer-based service that provides information to users or allows users to manipulate information. Usage note: Information services (IS) departments are typically responsible for deploying information technology.

information technology (IT)
A collective term for equipment, software, and other facilities used to process electronic information or provide information services.

Internet (the)
A global network that connects millions of computers in more than 100 countries for the exchange of data. The Internet is decentralized by design. Each Internet computer is independent of all others. Its operators can choose which Internet services to use and which of the computer's services to make available to the Internet community.

Internet Control Message Protocol (ICMP)
A control protocol strongly related to IP and TCP and used to convey a variety of control and error indications. (SNIA)

Internet Protocol (IP)
A protocol that provides connectionless best effort delivery of datagrams across heterogeneous physical networks. (SNIA)

IP
See Internet Protocol.

IT
See information technology.

J

JBOD
See just a bunch of disks.

just a bunch of disks (JBOD)
A collection of disks, usually in a common enclosure, that are not under central control such as that provided by a RAID controller.

L

local area network
A communications infrastructure designed to use dedicated wiring over a limited distance (typically a diameter of less than five kilometers) to connect a large number of intercommunicating nodes. Ethernet and token ring are the two most popular LAN technologies. *cf.* **wide area network** (SNIA)

logical unit (number) (LUN)
A partial address by which a virtual storage device is recognized and accessed on an I/O bus or storage network.

LUN
See logical unit (number).

M

mainframe
A large computer capable of supporting hundreds, or even thousands, of users simultaneously.

migration
The act of copying data objects from one storage device to another and deleting them from their original location. Hierarchical storage managers migrate files from primary to secondary (usually tape or optical disk) storage, releasing primary storage capacity for other purposes and modifying file system metadata to indicate that file data can be located using a catalog and the file's primary storage space can be *purged*, or reallocated for other purposes. Volume managers and other virtualization control software also migrate segments of virtual storage capacity between physical devices to balance load or protect against gradually failing devices.

mirror
(1) A complete copy of a virtual block storage device's storage capacity, usually on a separate set of storage devices from other copies.
(2) The process of block virtualization by making two or more identical copies of the block address spaces of one or more striped or concatenated disks or LUNs.

mirroring
A storage virtualization technique in which two or more complete copies of a block storage device's storage capacity are kept in synchronization.

NAS
See network attached storage.

network attached storage (NAS)
Persistent data storage that is connected ("attached") to its clients via a network. The term network attached storage is almost always used to denote a class of storage devices that organize data in files and use file access protocols (CIFS and NFS) to communicate with clients.

network file system (NFS)
A client-server file access network protocol originally developed by Sun Microsystems Computer Corporation and commonly implemented for UNIX operating systems (although implementations exist for other operating systems). The IETF is responsible for the NFS standard.

NFS
See network file system.

P

pay-for-use model
A common payment model for utility services in which each customer is financially responsible for services used.

platform
A computer, operating system, and other middleware that collectively provide an environment in which IT services can be offered or applications can be run.

protocol
CONTEXT [Fibre Channel] [Network] [SCSI] A set of rules for using an interconnect or network so that information conveyed on the interconnect can be correctly interpreted by all parties to the communication. Protocols include such aspects of communication as data representation, data item ordering, message formats, message and response sequencing rules, block data transmission conventions, timing requirements, and so forth. (SNIA)

provisioning
Allocating a set of resources among a collection of individual users.

R

RAID
(1) Acronym for redundant array of inexpensive disks. An array of disk drives or other block storage devices that is virtualized by any of several forms of control software.
(2) Acronym for redundant array of independent disks. The original meaning of the acronym RAID. Coined by researchers led by David Patterson at the University of California at Berkeley in the late 1980s.

RAID system
A storage system capable of using RAID techniques to virtualize disk storage.

recovery time
The time required to restore operation of an information service after a failure or disaster.

redeployment
The reuse of a set of storage resources that had previously been used for another purpose. Online storage is often redeployed when it is replaced by newer technology.

Reference Model-Open Distributed Processing (RM-ODP)
A standard of the International Standards Organization (ISO). RM-ODP defines a reference model or framework of architectural concepts for distributed system architectures.

replication
See data replication.

response time
The time between the making of a request for service and completion of the request's execution. Response time includes both queuing time while awaiting resources to process the request and execution time once the request is removed from the queue and execution begins. In an I/O system context, applications typically stall for the response time after issuing I/O requests, so response time is critical to application performance.

RM-ODP
See Reference Model-Open Distributed Processing.

rota
A roster of contact information that specifies the order in which individuals should be called upon to perform certain duties. Rotas are typically used in IT failure and disaster situations to identify the order in which individuals should be summoned to participate in various facets of the recovery process.

SAN
See storage area network.

satellite TV (SATV)
A broadband communications technology in which multiple television channels, as well as audio and data signals, are transmitted either one way or bidirectionally through a satellite distribution system.

SATV
See satellite TV.

scalability
The ability to accommodate growth in one dimension and provide proportional growth in another. For example, a storage system is scalable if growth in its capacity is accompanied by a corresponding growth in performance.

scaling
Exhibiting the property of scalability.

service-level agreement (SLA)
A contract between customer and service provider that defines the expectations for performance, availability, and other aspects dealing with the service.

service management

A stage in an enterprise's transition from conventional data processing to the IT utility model during which application SLAs are negotiated and executed. This stage introduces automated tools that discover, configure, pool, and allocate storage and servers, as well as application modeling tools that make it possible to estimate resource requirements. The service management stage is ideal for introducing service delivery portals. The primary benefits at this stage are better alignment of IT with business objectives through service standardization and a self-service user culture.

SLA

See service-level agreement.

snapshot

A physical or virtual image of the contents of a virtual block storage device or file system as they exist at a single point in time. Snapshots are usually made at times when data is consistent, as for example, when applications are quiescent and data manager caches have been flushed.

source (device)

A virtual storage device whose contents are replicated to one or more target devices.

storage area network (SAN)

(1) A network whose primary purpose is the transfer of data between computer systems and storage elements and among storage elements. Abbreviated SAN. A SAN consists of a communication infrastructure, which provides physical connections, and a management layer, which organizes the connections, storage elements, and computer systems so that data transfer is secure and robust. The term SAN is usually (but not necessarily) identified with block I/O services rather than file access services.

(2) A storage system consisting of storage elements, storage devices, computer systems, and/or appliances, plus all control software, communicating over a network. (SNIA)

storage capacity

The number of bytes of data that a storage device or piece of media is capable of storing.

storage device
Any device that holds data persistently for retrieval or updating on demand. Storage devices may be physical, as disk drives and tape drives, or virtual, as LUNs presented by RAID systems or volume managers.

storage network
A network whose primary purpose is intercommunication between storage devices and application servers or between groups of storage devices.

storage system
A computer system whose primary function is the persistent storage and on-demand delivery of data.

storage virtualizer
A device or body of software that virtualizes storage. Server-based volume managers, RAID systems, and network storage appliances are all storage virtualizers.

switch
A network infrastructure device that interconnects storage clients (application servers), storage devices, and other switches. The distinguishing characteristics of a switch are the ability to establish and break momentary connections between pairs of devices and the ability to maintain multiple momentary connections between pairs of devices simultaneously.

system
Any entity that performs an identifiable and separable function. A system may be a component of another system, or it may itself be made up of other systems.

T

tape drive virtualization
The pooling of tape drives so that any drive from a pool can be assigned to satisfy a backup server's request for a tape drive. Tape drives may be virtualized by cooperating software modules running in each of the backup servers with access to the pool or by hardware components in a storage network that assign tape drives on demand to respond to network addresses that are "owned" by servers.

TCP/IP
See Transmission Control Protocol/Internet Protocol.

ticketing system
Synonym for workflow system.

tiered services
Functionally equivalent services delivered at different performance and availability levels for different costs.

transaction
A set of operations on data that collectively have business significance. The operations that comprise a transaction must be performed in their entirety for the data on which they operate to accurately reflect a business state. Database management systems implement transaction semantics for application-defined sets of database operations.

Transmission Control Protocol/Internet Protocol (TCP/IP)
The Internet connection oriented network transfer protocol. (SNIA)

UDDI
Acronym for Universal Description, Discovery, and Integration. The UDDI specification enables businesses to quickly, easily, and dynamically find and transact with one another. UDDI enables a business to describe its business and its services, discover other businesses that offer desired services, and integrate with these other businesses. For more information on UDDI, please visit http://www.uddi.org.

UDP
See User Datagram Protocol.

UNIX
A collective term for several commercially available computer operating systems with common origins and similar properties. Popular commercial examples of UNIX include Sun Microsystems' Solaris, Hewlett-Packard's HP-UX, and IBM's AIX. Although Linux has similar origins to these other UNIXes, it is generally not considered to be a UNIX variant.

User Datagram Protocol
An Internet protocol that provides connectionless datagram delivery service to applications. UDP over IP adds the ability to address multiple endpoints within a single network node to IP. (SNIA)

utility
A business that provides standardized essential services reliably enough that they can be taken for granted by consumers. A utility delivers its services over continuously available metered connections and finances itself by billing consumers in a way that reflects the cost of the services that they consume.

utility computing
The technologies, tools, and processes that collectively deliver to users and manage reliable, measurable IT services on a pay-per-use basis.

utility management
The final stage in an enterprise's transition from conventional data processing to a utility computing model. At this stage, IT becomes a true utility. Automation enables dynamic deployment of resources for optimal utilization amid changing needs. From a business alignment standpoint, the transition to a self-service user mentality should be complete. Accountability, including the ability to charge users for IT services if appropriate, should be mature.

utility model
An abstract model of the essential characteristics that make up a utility such as an electric, gas, CATV, or telephone company. The essential characteristics of the utility model are a small menu of standard services, a large community of potential users, payment for use, and automated service management.

VERITAS Cluster Server
A server clustering software suite offered by VERITAS that provides application failover, shared data, parallel application support, and single system image management of up to 32 servers of the same architecture.

VERITAS OpForce™
An automatic server provisioning software suite offered by VERITAS. With OpForce, servers can be rapidly deployed and provisioned. OpForce auto-discovers both deployed and newly added servers. OpForce runs on Solaris, Linux, and Windows platforms and provisions Solaris, AIX, Linux, and Windows platforms.

VERITAS SANPoint Control™
A storage network management software suite offered by VERITAS. SANPoint Control software provides centralized, proactive management of a network storage infrastructure, including policy, performance management, storage provisioning, and zoning.

VERITAS Volume Manager
A server-based storage virtualization software suite offered by VERITAS. Volume Manager relaxes the capacity, performance, and availability limitations of physical disk storage and enables online configuration, sharing, management, and performance optimization of online storage without interrupting data availability.

virtual storage device
An abstraction implemented in software whose behavior is sufficiently similar to that of a physical storage device that applications and data managers can use it as such. Also known as a volume.

virtualization
Abstraction of key properties of a physical device and presentation of those properties to users of the device. In information technology, disk and tape storage devices, servers, and network connections are commonly virtualized. Virtualization is most often implemented by software interposed between a device user and one or more physical devices that collectively provide virtual device behavior.

volume
Synonym for virtual storage device.

volume manager
A server-based block virtualization control software suite such as the VERITAS Volume Manager.

Web (the)
Short for the World Wide Web.

Web access
To visit a Web site.

Web Services Description Language (WSDL)
An XML format for describing network services as a set of endpoints operating on messages containing either document-oriented or procedure-oriented information.

wide area network
CONTEXT [Network] A communications network that is geographically dispersed and that includes telecommunications links. (SNIA)

Windows
Common parlance for any or all of Microsoft's Windows operating systems.

World Wide Web (WWW)
A collection of Internet servers that collectively distribute documents formatted in HTML. Web documents may include links to other documents, as well as graphic, audio, and video files. Not all Internet servers participate in the World Wide Web.

workflow
A description of a set of tasks and the order in which they must be performed to produce a desired result.

workflow system
A suite of computer programs that manage workflow. Workflow systems track work items through each step of execution, notifying the individuals responsible for each step when the previous step is complete and supplying them with data necessary to execute the steps for which they are responsible.

WSDL
See Web Services Description Language.

WWW
See World Wide Web.

Z

zone
(1) A set of port or device addresses in a storage network that are permitted to intercommunicate.
(2) A set of adjacent tracks on a disk drive, all of which are formatted to contain the same number of blocks.

zoning
A technique used in Fibre Channel storage networks to limit the set of attached devices with which other devices can communicate. Zoning is most often implemented in switches but can also be implemented by server-based software.

Index

D

E

F

G

H

I

V

W